ANGER FOR ADULTS

How To Overcome Anger, Manage Your Emotions, Conquer Impulsiveness And Achieve Self Control

By Summer Blodgett

CONTENTS

	Introduction	Pg 1
1	Understand your Anger and Mental Health	Pg 3
2	The Roots of the All Problems, Mental Disorder	Pg 20
3	The Importance of the Control	Pg 27
4	Social Anxiety Disorder	Pg 31
5	The 21 Daily Strategies	Pg 39
6	Awareness	Pg 52
7	Emotions!	Pg 62
8	Anger Management Classes	Pg 72
9	Get Out The Stress From Your Life	Pg 75
10	Keep Calm At Every Provocations	Pg 94
11	Breathing Therapy	Pg 114
12	Personality Disorder:	Pg 121

How To Recognize It

13 Meditation Techniques   Pg 126

14 Anger Management The Law   Pg 135

    Of Attraction Way

15 Life-Change   Pg 146

    Conclusion   Pg 151

INTRODUCTION

Anger is a fundamental emotion that everyone experiences from time to time. From a very early age, people learn to express anger by copying the angry behavior they see modeled around them, and by expressing angry behavior and seeing what they can get away with. As many cultures have an uneasy relationship with anger expression, many people are brought up to think that it is inappropriate to express anger directly; that it must not be tolerated; that it is always dangerous. Such people learn to distrust anger, to bottle it up and ignore it, to express it only in indirect ways or to use it as a weapon.

The idea that anger is dangerous is not without merit. Angry people are capable of great violence. However, while anger can certainly be abused, it is more than a simple destructive force. Anger is also a critically important part of what might be called the self-preservation and self-defense instincts. People who are incapable of getting angry are also incapable of standing up for themselves. It is important then that people learn how to express anger appropriately. People need to learn healthy and socially respectful ways to express angry feelings and to not to let anger get out of control to the point where it negatively affects relationships, employability, and health.

If you are reading this document, there is a good chance that you (or someone you care about) have an anger problem. An anger problem exists when people become dependent on anger as a primary means of expressing themselves; when they inappropriately use anger or the threat of violence as a weapon to get their way. Inappropriate and uncontrolled anger is harmful for both targets of anger and the angry person as well. Inappropriate anger destroys relationships, makes it difficult to hold down a job, and takes a heavy toll on angry people's physical and emotional health.

Help for anger problems exists in the form of anger management programs which are designed to help angry people learn and practice methods of bringing their anger under control.

This document reviews what is known about anger and anger management. It starts with a discussion of the nature of anger and anger's effects on people's social, emotional and physical welfare. Reasons and motivations for pursuing anger management are discussed, and then specific techniques used in anger management courses are described. The document concludes by describing ways motivated people can use anger management techniques to learn to control their anger so as to protect their health, promote the quality of their relationships and become more socially effective.

☐

CHAPTER 1: UNDERSTAND YOUR ANGER AND MENTAL HEALTH

Anger is a basic human emotion that is experienced by all people. Typically triggered by an emotional hurt, anger is usually experienced as an unpleasant feeling that occurs when we think we have been injured, mistreated, opposed in our long-held views, or when we are faced with obstacles that keep us from reaching personal goals.

The experience of anger varies widely; how often anger occurs, how intensely it is felt, and how long it lasts are different for each person. People also vary in how easily they get angry (known as their anger threshold), as well as how comfortable they are with feeling angry. Some people are always getting angry while others seldom feel angry. Some people are very aware of their anger, while others fail to recognize anger when it occurs. Some experts suggest that the average adult gets angry about once a day and annoyed or peeved about three times a day. Other anger management experts suggest that getting angry fifteen times a day is more likely a realistic average. Regardless of how often we actually experience anger, it is a common and unavoidable emotion.

Anger can be constructive or destructive. When well-managed, anger or annoyance has very few hurtful health or relationship consequences. At its roots, anger is a signal to you that something in your environment isn't right. It captures your attention and motivates you to take action to correct that wrong thing. How you end up handling the anger signal has very important consequences for your overall health and welfare, however. When you express anger, your actions trigger others to become defensive and angry too. Blood pressures raises and stress hormones flow. Violence can then follow. You may develop a reputation as a dangerous 'loose cannon' whom no one wants to be around.

Out of control anger alienates friends, co-workers and family members. It also has a clear relationship with health problems and early death. Hostile, aggressive anger not only increases your risk for an early death but also your risk for social isolation, which itself is a major risk factor for serious illness and death. These are but two of many reasons why learning to properly manage anger is a good idea.

4

Psychology of Anger

The physiological aspects of anger are very interesting as the effects on the body are very noticeable but out of our control in many ways. Even if we are good at controlling our external display of anger we may still be unable to control the physical response that occurs within our body. The physiology of anger has been studied for many years by many different groups of people who all agree that overall the person to be the most negatively effected by anger is the person who is experiencing the anger.

Anger is a natural and mostly automatic response to pain of one form or another (physical or emotional). Anger can occur when people don't feel well, feel rejected, feel threatened, or experience some loss. The type of pain does not matter; the important thing is that the pain experienced is unpleasant. Because anger never occurs in isolation but rather occurs after pain feelings, it is often characterized as a 'secondhand' emotion.

Pain alone is not enough to cause anger. Anger occurs when pain is combined with some anger-triggering thought. Thoughts that can trigger anger include personal assessments, assumptions, evaluations, or interpretations of situations that makes people think that someone else is attempting (consciously or not) to hurt them. In this sense, anger is a social emotion; You always have a target that your anger is directed against (even if that target is yourself). Feelings of pain, combined with anger-triggering thoughts, motivate you to take action, face threats and defend yourself by striking out against the target you think is causing you pain.

Anger can also be a substitute emotion. By this, we mean that sometimes people make themselves angry so that they don't have to feel pain. People change their feelings of pain into anger because it feels better to be angry than it does to be in pain. This changing of pain into anger may be done consciously or unconsciously.

Being angry rather than simply in pain has a number of advantages, primarily among them distraction. People in pain generally think about their pain. However, angry people think about harming those who have caused pain. Part of the changing of pain into anger involves an attention shift - from self-focus to other-focus. Anger thus temporarily protects people from having to recognize and deal with their painful real feelings; you get to worry about getting back at the people you're angry with instead. Making yourself angry can help you to hide the reality that you find a situation frightening or that you feel vulnerable.

Becoming angry also creates a feeling of righteousness, power and being better than others that is not present when someone is merely in pain. When you are angry, you are angry with cause. "The people who have hurt me are wrong – they should be punished" is the common refrain. It is very rare that someone will get angry with someone they do not think has harmed them in some significant fashion.

The definition of whether someone's anger is a problem often turns on whether or not other people agree with them that their anger, and the actions they take in the name of their anger, is justified. Angry people most always feel that their anger is justified. However, other people don't always agree. The social judgment of anger creates real consequences for the angry person. An angry person may feel justified in committing an angry, aggressive action, but if a judge or jury of peers do not see it that way, that angry person may still go to jail. If a boss doesn't agree that anger expressed towards a customer is justified, a job may still be lost. If a spouse doesn't agree that anger was justified, a marriage may have problems.

Whether justified or unjustified, the seductive feeling of righteousness associated with anger offers a powerful temporary boost to self-esteem. It is more satisfying to feel angry than to acknowledge the painful feelings associated with vulnerability. You can use anger to convert feelings of vulnerability and helplessness into feelings of control and power. Some people develop an unconscious habit of transforming almost all of their vulnerable feelings into anger so they can avoid having to deal with them. The problem becomes that even when anger distracts you from the fact that you feel vulnerable, you still at some level feel vulnerable. Anger cannot make pain disappear – it only distracts you from it. Anger generally does not resolve or address the problems that made you feel fearful or vulnerable in the first place, and it can create new problems, including social and health issues.

The Biological Process

Emotional disturbance can cause a disruption to many of the chemical balances in the body. The same chemicals are involved in regulating many of our biological processes and keeping us healthy. These chemicals are called adrenalin and noradrenalin which surge when we begin to feel angry. The physical result can cause our respiration rate to increase as our oxygen demand becomes greater due to our blood pressure and heart rate increase. Our body can shake as our blood sugar plummets and our pancreas tries to keep up with demand. When these reactions are caused very often or to a high degree, long term damage can result. In some instances when someone becomes very angry very quickly the physical reactions can cause the blood to clot very quickly and this clot can travel to the heart or lungs causing rapid and potentially lethal complications especially when combined with a drop in blood oxygen levels. It is not just our circulation and respiration that is affected by anger as our gastro-intestinal organs may also suffer. Anger can cause a rise in stomach acids which can cause irritable bowel and diarrhoea along with a susceptibility to stomach ulcers as the acids attack the lining of the stomach.

People who are continually angry, risk having long term problems with blood pressure and may even be more susceptible to angina attacks or breathing problems. It is also possible that they may have an increased likelihood to suffer from panic attacks.Due to these physiological responses, it is important that we learn to cope with our anger in a way that is not going to cause us harm.When we feel ourselves becoming physically affected by a surge of anger we must learn to exert some control over our response and behaviour which will help the internal chemical reactions lessen in severity.

Anger can be a very powerful emotion causing severe physiological changes to occur which can be dangerous to health. In order to prevent anger being detrimental to health we must learn ways of lessening the chance of becoming angry or indeed how we mange and control anger when we do experience it.

What Causes Anger Problems?

Feelings of anger arise due to how we interpret and react to certain situations. Everyone has their own triggers for what makes them angry, but some common ones include situations in which we feel:

- Threatened or attacked

- Frustrated or powerless

- Like we're being treated unfairly.

People can interpret situations differently, so a situation that makes you feel very angry may not make someone else feel angry at all (for example, other reactions could include annoyance, hurt or amusement). But just because we can interpret things differently, it doesn't mean that you're interpreting things 'wrong' if you get angry. How you interpret and react to a situation can depend on lots of factors in your life, including:

- Your childhood and upbringing

- Past experiences

- Current circumstances

- Life Events

- Thinking Styles

- Behavioral Explanations

- Evolutionary Reasons

- Biological Reasons

Whether your anger is about something that happened in the past or something that's going on right now, thinking about how and why we interpret and react to situations can help us learn how to cope with our emotions better. It can also help us find productive strategies to handle our anger.

Your Childhood And Upbringing: How we learn to cope with angry feelings is often influenced by our upbringing. Many people are given messages about anger as children that may make it harder to manage it as an adult. For example:

• You may have grown up thinking that it's always okay to act out your anger aggressively or violently, and so you didn't learn how to understand and manage your angry feelings. This could mean you have angry outbursts whenever you don't like the way someone is behaving, or whenever you are in a situation you don't like.

• You may have been brought up to believe that you shouldn't complain, and may have been punished for expressing anger as a child. This could mean that you tend to suppress your anger and it becomes a long-term problem, where you react inappropriately to new situations you're not comfortable with.

• You may have witnessed your parents' or other adults' anger when it was out of control, and learned to think of anger as something that is destructive and terrifying. This could mean that you now feel afraid of your own anger and don't feel safe expressing your feelings when something makes you angry. Those feelings might then surface at another unconnected time, which may feel hard to explain.

Past Experiences: If you've experienced particular situations in the past that made you feel angry (either as a child or more recently as an adult) but you weren't able to safely express your anger at the time, you might still be coping with those angry feelings now. This might also mean that you now find certain situations particularly challenging, and more likely to make you angry. Sometimes your present feeling of anger may not only be about the current situation but may also be related to a past experience, which can mean that the anger you are feeling in the present is at a level that reflects your past situation. Becoming aware of this can help us to find ways of responding to situations in the present in a safer and less distressed way.

Current Circumstances: If you're dealing with a lot of other problems in your life right now, you might find yourself feeling angry more easily than usual, or getting angry at unrelated things. If there's a particular situation that's making you feel angry, but you don't feel able to express your anger directly or resolve it, then you might find you express that anger at other times. Anger can also be a part of grief. If you've lost someone important to you, it can be hugely difficult to cope with all the conflicting things you might be feeling.

Life Events: There may be certain situations which are more likely to trigger an angry reaction from you. Being exposed to a particular scenario or environment might put you on high alert. For example, some people find that they are much more likely to become angry whilst driving.

Thinking Styles: Our interpretation and thoughts about a situation can result in an angry outburst. Especially how we perceive the intentions of other people and the potential consequences to ourselves. Situations in which we feel wronged in some way can be particularly difficult. Also where an injustice has been done that we feel is unacceptable. Our understanding of anger may also influence our reaction. Our beliefs about anger can change the way that we express or control our anger. For example, if we consider that anger must be expressed and not 'bottled up'. We may not have considered making attempts to manage emotions in a more appropriate and sensitive way.

Behavioral Explanations: You might find it difficult to sit with and tolerate frustration. This may be due to your social experiences. Also, what you have come to consider as being normal and acceptable behavior. You may not have had opportunities to learn effective ways of managing and expressing emotions. A pattern of angry behavior can build up. This can become more and more difficult to overcome. In reality, it is likely that a combination of all these factors influence someone's anger. However, in some ways it is less important to know what causes anger, and more important to know what stops us moving past it.

Evolutionary Reasons: It is also possible that people develop anger issues because of evolutionary factors. To understand this, it is worth considering that humans are generally a sociable species who tend to thrive in the company of others. Because of this, it makes sense that people prefer to avoid upsetting others and ultimately being rejected. It, therefore, seems plausible that socially anxious people are simply slightly oversensitive to being negatively evaluated due to the disadvantages this brings. This could explain why socially anxious people go out of their way not to offend others.

Biological Reasons: It has also been suggested that anger has familial ties. In other words, if someone in your immediate family has anger issues, there is a higher chance that you will have similar personality traits. It is therefore thought that our genetic make-up plays a role in the levels of anger we experience.

Suppressing Anger

It is probably true that we all suppress anger at some point, for example when we are at work and we do not agree with a colleague or senior member of staff, we sometimes get angry but feel unable to express it, so we suppress it. For most of us this is not going to be a problem as usually the issue is fairly minor or is forgotten about or reflected upon. However some people may have had extremely traumatic events happen in their life that they have never been able to confront, control or even admit to; in these instances emotional responses can be hidden deep in the mind. A lot of these people will not allow their mind to process this information and it can become buried and almost consciously forgotten about. Our sub-conscious is a very powerful medium and will usually not allow us to carry this behaviour on forever and eventually the suppressed anger may re-surface.

Those who have suppressed their anger for many years may be doing themselves a lot of harm. We all get angry and most of deal with quite well at the time of incidence, but some people with chronic anger, or anger over issues in their past may suppress as a way of managing it; this is not necessarily the best anger management process.Over time this anger will find other ways of being expressed most commonly it turns back onto the angry person causing them to harm themselves in some way.Often this harmful behaviour manifests as alcohol abuse, drug abuse, self-harm or self-depreciation. Not only can these issues be seriously bad for health and potentially life-threatening, they are a lot more difficult to treat, more so than the various points of anger that have been allowed to build-up.

Suppressing anger can also have a detrimental effect on health and biological processes that are outside of our conscious control, and can result in some very serious illnesses and complaints.Doctors have research the effects of suppressing anger and most agree that over time you can irreversibly damage your heart muscle and cardiac function; in fact it can lead to heart disease which potentially threatens life.Keeping emotions bottled-up and hidden in our own minds can be very difficult and take a lot of energy and work even if we do not realise that this is occurring. This inadvertently causes our blood pressure to rise which means the heart has to work harder to achieve the same degree of circulation as it did with lower blood pressure. In order to achieve this, the lungs must try and keep up with the oxygen demand that will also have increased. If the body has to maintain this level of function it will become weary over time and start to deteriorate as it struggles to cope.

If we continually suppress our anger, eventually we will become mentally exhausted and find ways of coping with this. If we fill our minds full of emotions that have not been processed we will eventually be less able to achieve even the most common and basic tasks. It is possible that suppressed anger can cause the person to have difficulty dealing with everyday life and find it hard to separate fact from fiction.

Suppressing anger on a long term basis can be very bad for both mental and physical health. This does not mean that we should allow outbursts of anger, or sudden, abusive behaviour that we cannot control, but it does mean that we should find new anger management methods as soon as anger presents.

What Keeps An Anger Problem Going?

There may be a noticeable pattern to what happens before and after an angry episode. For example, whilst driving, looking after the children or whenever you're talking about money. It might be that we are getting into the habit of getting angry in such contexts. This might be difficult to break.

There may be consequences to angry behavior; both costs and benefits. Many people recognize that angry behavior can achieve short-term gain. For example, getting your own way, or having others respect your status. It can also be associated with significant long-term costs, such as damaged relationships. Considering these for yourself might encourage a change or convince you that you need to take action.

When looking more closely at what prevents us from overcoming anger problems, it becomes clear that our behavior, thoughts, feelings and physical sensations all interact and combine to keep our problems with anger going.

Anger can be an incredibly destructive emotion. It is an emotion that is important for us to understand.

Reasons For Understanding Anger

Anger is a Fact of Life: One of the most fundamental aspects of being a person is that we were created in God's image. Part of what it means to be made in

God's image is that we, like God, have a variety of emotions and are able to experience the emotions of others. One of these emotions is anger. What exactly is anger? Anger is a strong feeling of irritation or displeasure. When we experience anger, our mind and our body prepares us to act. Anger involves physical and emotional energy. It is up to us whether we use that energy in constructive ways or to abuse ourselves and/or those that we love. It is up to us whether we use that energy in constructive ways or to abuse ourselves and/or those that we love.

Anger is a Frequently Experienced Emotion: The emotion of anger is experienced much more frequently than most people would like to admit. When we begrudge or disdain others, or when we are annoyed, repulsed, irritated, frustrated, offended or cross, we are probably experiencing some form of anger. The results of research, as well as our own experience, suggest that most couples experience the emotion of anger a minimum of 8-10 times a day... and that's before they have kids.

Anger is One of the Most Powerful Emotions: The emotion of anger can provide tremendous energy to right wrongs and change things for the good. But when we allow it to control us, it can lead to negative destructive actions such as emotional, verbal or even physical abuse and violence. In any intimate relationship, there will be times when you will be hurt or wronged. When that happens, anger can easily distort our perspective, block our ability to love, and thus limit our ability to see things clearly.

Anger is a Secondary Emotion: Anger is a secondary emotion that is usually experienced in response to a primary emotion such as hurt, frustration, and fear. Anger can be an almost automatic response to any kind of pain. It is the emotion most of us feel shortly after we have been hurt. When your spouse corrects or talks down to you in public, it hurts, and you may respond to them in anger. At the moment it may be the only emotion that we are aware of, yet it is rarely the only one we have experienced. Below the surface, there are almost always other, deeper emotions that need to be identified and acknowledged.

Unhealthy Anger has Tremendous Potential for Harm: Most of us have, at one time or another, been pushed so hard and become so angry that we could have, or indeed have, become violent. I recently came across some sobering statistics that clearly demonstrate the potential harm of anger out of control:

• 10 million children were beaten by angry parents, two-thirds were under the age of 3

• 60% of all homicides were committed by people who knew the victim

• 27% of all policemen killed are killed breaking up domestic arguments

19

• More than 70% of all murderers don't have a criminal record

One psychiatrist interviewed more than 100 inmates convicted of murder and concluded that most were not angry people. In most cases, they had stuffed their emotions and allowed their anger to build and build, and in these cases, they were finally expressed in an out-of-control and violent way.

Healthy Anger has Tremendous Potential for Good: For most people, the emotion of anger is considered negative, a problem, something to be eliminated or solved. What we so often fail to see is that every problem is really an opportunity in disguise... an opportunity to learn, to grow, to mature, to be used of God to make significant changes for the good.

Anger is a Signal: Anger is an emotion that God can use to get our attention and make us more aware of opportunities to learn, to grow, to deepen, to mature, and to make significant changes for the good. Anger, like love, is an emotion that has tremendous potential for both good and evil. That's why it is so important for us to understand it.

▢

CHAPTER 2: THE ROOTS OF THE ALL PROBLEMS, MENTAL DISORDER

If you look down the symptom list of various mental illnesses, you'll see "anger" there. Anger is connected with depression, anxiety, bipolar disorder, ADHD, personality disorders and others. Why is anger a symptom of mental illness? For the most part, people without mental health problems aren't carrying a lot of anger inside over a prolonged period of time. They also have the capacity to control their anger. For those with a mental health condition, anger can be simmering below the surface ready to bubble up at a moment's notice.

There's also the issue of depression and impulsivity. When a person is depressed, many times they don't care how they come across. And with impulsivity, a lack of control, a person may just blurt out their feelings and not think about the ramifications.

It might be different to how the people around them think and act, but for the person with the mental health problem, these feelings are real. Just like physical illness, mental health problems can happen to anyone and people can recover from and manage. Mental health problems are common and anyone can experience one. Some are more severe than others, and some will have more noticeable symptoms. In most cases, they are manageable and people are able to live happy and successful lives.

What Causes Mental Disorder Problems?

Mental health problems may affect a person from any religion, culture, economic background or nationality. There are a number of factors that are associated with mental health problems.

Some of these factors may include:

Family History - If a family member has a mental health difficulty, others may be at higher risk.

Chemical Balance - An imbalance of chemicals (called neurotransmitters) in the brain can cause symptoms of a mental illness to emerge. Most drugs used to manage mental health difficulties try to correct this balance. There is also research that suggests the behavior itself can cause the chemical change in the brain (as opposed to the chemical imbalance simply always being there).

Stressful Life Events - Things in life that cause stress, or an experience such as grief or loss, experiencing violence or a traumatic accident may trigger mental health problems.

Drugs - Research has shown that using drugs may lead to mental health problems. For example, there has been a link between psychosis and the heavy use of marijuana and amphetamines.

Different Types Of Mental Disorder Problems

There are many terms used to describe mental health problems. This is an explanation of some of the common terms used.

Depression - When someone feels sad and down for a period of time that is longer than a couple of weeks they may be depressed. People experiencing depression may experience some or all of:

- Feelings of hopelessness or helplessness

- Loss of interest in what they usually enjoy

- A lack of energy

- Changes in sleeping and eating patterns

- Crying a lot for no reason

- Feeling anxious.

If someone is experiencing one or a number of these things, seeking help is important. Your GP is a good first step and they may refer you to a psychiatrist or help you themselves. A psychologist is also a specialist who can help you work through depression.

Psychosis - If someone becomes very confused and appears out of touch with everyone else's perception of the world, they may be experiencing a psychotic episode. When someone is experiencing a psychosis they may:

• Have hallucinations

• Hear voices that may not be heard by anyone else

• Have false beliefs known as delusions

• Experience paranoia

• Have strange and disorganized thinking

• Have strange and disorganized behavior

• Have difficulty speaking coherently

• May appear quite flat.

Some drugs such as hallucinogens, marijuana, and amphetamines may trigger a psychotic episode. Treatment of psychosis usually involves medication, and if someone is experiencing a psychotic episode, it is important they seek help from a doctor, psychiatrist or a clinical psychologist. Friends and family can also provide support. Achieving stability after a psychotic episode may take some time.

Schizophrenia - Schizophrenia is a serious mental illness characterized by disturbances in a person's thoughts, perceptions, emotions, and behavior. It affects approximately one in every hundred people worldwide and first onset commonly occurs in adolescence or early adulthood, although it can also occur later in life.

There are a number of signs and symptoms that are characteristic of schizophrenia. However, the expression of these symptoms varies greatly from one individual to another. No one symptom is common to all people and not everyone who displays these symptoms has schizophrenia (as some physical conditions can mimic schizophrenia). Generally speaking, symptoms are divided into two groups, 'active' symptoms (also referred to as 'positive' or psychotic symptoms) that reflect new or unusual forms of thought and behavior, such as delusions or hallucinations. 'Passive' symptoms (also referred to as 'negative' symptoms) reflect a loss of previous feelings and abilities.

Schizophrenia does not mean someone has more than one personality or 'split personalities'. With medication and support, schizophrenia can be managed. Having the support of family and friends may also be very helpful. The earlier people receive help for schizophrenia, the greater the chance of a better outcome.

Anxiety - There are many forms of anxiety disorders that can stop people from doing what they want to do. Some people have sudden unexplained panic attacks that can seem out of their control. Some people experience phobias like agoraphobia (fear of being in an open space).

Other people become anxious about something in particular. This can lead to obsessive behavior causing them to check and recheck things, for example: having to go home to check that they turned off the cooker. People who experience high levels of anxiety can learn to manage and reduce their anxiety levels. A form of therapy called Cognitive Behavioral Therapy has been shown to be really effective in managing anxiety. Look at anxiety for more information.

Attention Deficit Disorder - When someone has problems concentrating and staying focused on tasks, they may have an attention deficit disorder. The condition may have started in early childhood. They may be easily distracted, excessively active, or have a tendency to go off into daydreams more than others.

People with attention deficit disorders find situations like paying attention in class particularly difficult, and this can lead to conflict with teachers or other authority figures. They may feel like the world is against them because of the conflicts that arise due to their inability to concentrate.

People with attention deficit disorders may have a lot of energy and become involved in many activities that can be positive. Young people experiencing attention deficit disorder may need to be helped by their family and school, as well as receiving good medical support.

After proper medical assessment, medication may be helpful in managing symptoms.

Eating Disorders - Eating disorder is the term used to describe a group of illnesses where someone has a distorted view of body image with a preoccupation around eating, food and weight. There are a number of different eating disorders including Anorexia Nervosa, Bulimia Nervosa, and Binge eating disorder.

If someone has an eating disorder, it is a good idea for them to get help as soon as possible. This help may come from their local doctor who may then refer them to a psychiatrist or other mental health professional.

If you or someone you know is having a tough time with your mental health, check out face-to-face help for information on who to talk to and how to get support. There's also loads of support available online or over the phone.

⁇

CHAPTER 3: THE IMPORTANCE OF THE CONTROL

Do you have a short fuse or find yourself getting into frequent arguments and fights? Anger is a normal, healthy emotion, but when chronic, explosive anger spirals out of control, it can have serious consequences for your relationships, your health, and your state of mind.

With insight about the real reasons for your anger and these anger management tools, you can learn to keep your temper from hijacking your life.

You might think that venting your anger is healthy, that the people around you are too sensitive, that your anger is justified, or that you need to show your fury to get respect. But the truth is that anger is much more likely to damage your relationships, impair your judgment, get in the way of success, and have a negative impact on the way people see you.

You Do/Say Things You End Up Regretting

I have a confession. I don't know how to express my anger "normally". I usually keep quiet and after a long time – months, years even – the smallest thing can set me off; and then the anger comes out like a raging storm. Then I end up saying hurtful things that have been on my mind for so long but have not said out loud because I knew they would cut deep and not help resolve the issue. I even end up saying things I don't really mean – just because I cannot control my anger at that point. The result? An even bigger problem where the issue/s between the parties involved escalate.

Here's another (hypothetical) scenario: an individual who gets angry easily and finds himself in the same position I just described. The difference is that this person is caught in the vicious cycle of getting angry and behaving in an inappropriate manner: being verbally rude perhaps, throwing things around maybe, and the likes. At the end of the day, however, the person regrets his behavior, whether or not he admits it to others. Two different people, two different ways of handling anger. Same result: hurting those around them and themselves as well.

You Suffer Physically And Mentally

Being always angry may work for Dr. Bruce Banner, but in real life, that strategy might very well be the death of you – literally. Whether you hold it in till you explode, or you explode all the time, your body is under a lot of stress – and we know what extreme and/or constant stress can do to your health.

High blood pressure, hyperacidity and headaches. These are only some of the things that you can physically suffer from if you don't control your anger.

Then there is the mental/emotional aspect. Being unable to control your anger can lead to guilt, among many other things. In turn, that can again translate to physical issues like lack of sleep, fatigue, and other illnesses. These two main reasons alone should be enough to convince you that you need to find a way (or ways) to control your anger unless you want to suffer the consequences all your life and live an unhappy existence.

Anger Is Contagious

Imagine a husband who comes home from work, angry and shouts at his wife. The wife gets upset because she doesn't understand her husband's reaction, and yells at her kid. Out of frustration, the child kicks the dog which then runs outside and bites the mailman. As you can see, anger can sometimes be extremely contagious. If one of these people had been able to stop and consider his/her actions, the chain of reaction could have been prevented.

Becoming More Empathetic

Anger Management helps you develop empathy for others, which in turn helps you to better understand the other party. Many times, anger builds up because the parties involved do not care to see the situation from the other person's point of view. When you start developing empathy for the other person and try to see life from their perspective, you will find there is no room for conflict.

Building Better Relationships

Many individuals, who have serious anger issues, begin to avoid those they love most when they realize they are hurting them with their anger. Since those we love most are closest to us, they are often the first victims of our out of control anger.

Gaining New Insight

Anger Management affords you an opportunity to learn more about your anger, its root cause, and triggers. The way you feel and express yourself in your day to day life can most often be connected to feelings and emotions that you have experienced in your past. When this connection is explored during therapy, you will begin to gain new insight which will help you be more aware of your feelings and learn to better understand the nature of your anger and its origin.

Developing Better Judgment

Left uncontrolled, anger leads to poor decision making. In therapy, you will learn to skills to help you to better manage your anger, which will allow you to use better judgment and have more control over your impulses.

Experiencing Less Stress

The ability to better manage stress will be an immediate benefit of anger management. Experiencing less stress, you will discover that it becomes more easy to avoid situations that otherwise would become stressful.

Replacing Aggressive Communication With Assertive

Most times anger and angry situations may have been avoided if the parties involved knew how to communicate better. Most problems can be solved when those involved know how to properly communicate assertively. If you do not know how to properly assert yourself, angry behavior is often used in its place.

Knowing Your Responsibility

In anger management, you will to develop an ability to recognize what you are responsible for in how you think of anger, such as when you are the cause of a problem and when you are innocent. When you recognize you are not at fault, you know how to keep a situation calm, yet assign blame to where it rightly should be.

⏹

CHAPTER 4: SOCIAL ANXIETY DISORDER

Social anxiety disorder, also known as social phobia, is a mental illness. It belongs to a group of mental illnesses called anxiety disorders. People with social anxiety disorder feel very nervous and uncomfortable in social situations like meeting new people. Or they might feel very anxious when they have to do something in front of other people, like talking in a meeting. Some people feel very anxious in both situations.

People with social anxiety disorder often feel like they will say or do the wrong thing. Or they might think that other people will look down on them and think poorly of them because they're "strange" or "stupid." It's important to know that adults with social anxiety disorder recognize that they feel too anxious, but they may not be able to control it.

Some people may have a panic attack or feel some physical signs of anxiety when they're facing a social situation. Common physical signs of anxiety include stomach aches, shallow breathing, sweating or feeling hot flashes, feeling like your heart is racing, feeling tightness in your chest, feeling tense and feeling shaky.

Social anxiety disorder can have a very negative effect on your well-being and quality of life. The illness can cause a lot of problems in your relationships with partners, family, and friends. It can also seriously affect your school or work life. You may avoid certain careers or fields of study, avoid contributing your ideas, turn down promotions, drop out of school or take many days off because you feel so anxious. Some people with social anxiety disorder fear one or just a few specific social situations. Others fear a wide range of social situations.

Common social anxiety triggers include:

- Meeting new people

- Making small talk

- Public speaking

- Performing on stage

- Being the center of attention

- Being watched while doing something

- Being teased or criticized

- Talking with "important" people or authority figures

- Being called on in class

- Going on a date

- Speaking up in a meeting

- Using public restrooms

- Taking exams

- Eating or drinking in public

- Making phone calls

- Attending parties or other social gatherings

Signs And Symptoms Of Social Anxiety Disorder

Just because you occasionally get nervous in social situations doesn't mean you have social anxiety disorder or social phobia. Many people feel shy or self-conscious on occasion, yet it doesn't get in the way of their everyday functioning. Social anxiety disorder, on the other hand, does interfere with your normal routine and causes tremendous distress.

For example, it's perfectly normal to get the jitters before giving a speech. But if you have social anxiety, you might worry for weeks ahead of time, call in sick to get out of it or start shaking so bad during the speech that you can hardly speak.

Emotional signs and symptoms of social anxiety disorder:

• Excessive self-consciousness and anxiety in everyday social situations

• Intense worry for days, weeks, or even months before an upcoming social situation

• Extreme fear of being watched or judged by others, especially people you don't know

• Fear that you'll act in ways that will embarrass or humiliate yourself

• Fear that others will notice that you're nervous

Physical signs and symptoms:

• Red face, or blushing

• Shortness of breath

• Upset stomach, nausea (i.e. butterflies)

• Trembling or shaking (including shaky voice)

• Racing heart or tightness in chest

• Sweating or hot flashes

- Feeling dizzy or faint

Behavioral signs and symptoms:

- Avoiding social situations to a degree that limits your activities or disrupts your life

- Staying quiet or hiding in the background in order to escape notice and embarrassment

- A need to always bring a buddy along with you wherever you go

- Drinking before social situations in order to soothe your nerves

Who Does It Affect?

Social anxiety disorder is one of the most common types of anxiety disorders, and one of the most common mental illnesses. About 8% of people will experience symptoms of social anxiety disorder at some point in their life. Without treatment, social anxiety disorder can last for a long time. Unfortunately, many people never seek help for social anxiety disorder. There are some groups of people at higher risk of experiencing social anxiety disorder:

- Age - Social phobia usually starts during the child or teen years, usually at about age 13. A doctor can tell that a person has social phobia if the person has had symptoms for at least six months. Without treatment, social phobia can last for many years or a lifetime. The majority of people with social anxiety disorder say that their symptoms started before they were 18

• Women - Women are more likely to experience social anxiety disorder than men

• Other mental illnesses or substance use disorder - Many people with social anxiety disorder have other mental illness like depression, panic disorder, bulimia nervosa (an eating disorder) and substance use disorders. However, social anxiety seems to appear before other mental illnesses.

What Prevents You Overcoming Social Anxiety?

Unhelpful Thoughts: People's unhelpful thoughts and predictions make it more difficult for them to overcome their social anxiety. Socially anxious people often hold unhelpful thoughts about themselves and their ability in social situations (e.g. I'm dull; I'm weird). This, of course, lowers their confidence and makes it harder to become involved in social situations. This, in turn, means they rarely get the chance to test out their social skills and prove they can interact well.

Unhelpful thoughts also typically play a damaging role just prior to people entering social environments as they predict they will perform poorly (e.g. I'll have nothing to say). Similarly, unhelpful thoughts influence people during social situations (e.g. I'm making a fool of myself), as they assume they are not coming across well. To make matters worse, after social situations, people often analyze their performance and assume they have performed poorly. When considering these factors, it is easy to see how unhelpful thoughts stop people overcoming their social anxiety.

Avoidance: As mentioned earlier, socially anxious people tend to avoid social contact whenever possible. If they cannot avoid it, they tend to try and escape it as quickly as possible. Although this is a very understandable way of coping with social anxiety, it is actually one of the main reasons that people find it hard to overcome. This is because by avoiding social situations, people stop themselves having positive experiences that could disprove some of their unhelpful thoughts. Furthermore, the longer someone avoids a social situation, the more daunting it becomes and it is increasingly difficult to face.

Using 'Safety Behaviors': Often, the only time that socially anxious people feel comfortable in social settings, is when they use what is known as 'safety behavior'. Examples of 'safety behaviors' include: trying to stay in the background on social occasions; remaining quiet during group conversations; sticking closely besides those they know well; avoiding eye contact or drinking alcohol for extra courage. Basically, a 'safety behavior' is anything people do to try and make it easier to cope in social situations.

Although such safety behaviors help people feel slightly better at the time, they are actually unhelpful strategies in the longer term. This is because, like avoidance, 'safety behaviors' stop people from having the opportunity to prove that they can cope well, without putting such precautions into place. Instead 'safety behaviors' allow people to put their successes down to other factors (e.g. I only achieved that because my friend was with me). Similarly, by remaining quiet during conversations, they never have the opportunity to show that they would have coped well had they became more involved. As a result, people's confidence remains low and their social anxiety remains. A final point worth noting is that 'safety behaviors' can result in what is known as self-fulfilling prophecies. For example, by staying quiet in social situations, people may come across as 'distant' and others may respond by making less of an effort. As a result, their beliefs that they can't mix well remain in place.

Increased Self Focus: People who are socially anxious often spend a lot of time concentrating on their own bodily sensations during social interactions. Unfortunately, this too plays a part in keeping social anxiety going. For example, people often spend time trying to judge whether they are sweating, stammering, shaking or blushing during social situations. Although they do so in the hope of being reassured that they are not noticeably anxious, this strategy actually just makes things much worse. This is because people tend to overestimate how visible their anxiety is and this, of course, makes them feel even more self-conscious. Also, by focusing on themselves, it means that they are not fully focusing on the conversations going on around them. This makes it more difficult to join in properly and strengthens their beliefs that they are no good in such situations. It is likely that a combination of these factors play a role in ensuring people's social anxiety continues.

CHAPTER 5: THE 21 DAILY STRATEGIES

Although we think we are driven to anger by external factors, the emotion itself is really a function of our own interpretation of an event or situation. For example, a bad driver who cuts you off in busy traffic isn't the cause of your anger; how you choose to react to the driver is what determines whether you get angry or not. For this reason, researchers argue that angry feelings occur due to angry thoughts. It is therefore up to you to choose how you process external stimuli that can trigger angry thoughts which lead to angry feelings.

This is where anger management techniques can help. Using specific strategies, you can better predict and understand your own anger. So let's take a look at 21 proven strategies that can help you manage your anger in a positive manner.

Identify What Triggers Your Anger

If you've gotten into the habit of losing your temper, it can be helpful to take stock of the things that trigger your anger. Long lines, traffic jams, snarky comments from a friend, or being overtired are just a few things that might shorten your fuse. That's not to say you should blame people or external circumstances for your inability to keep your cool. But, understanding the things that trigger your anger can help you plan accordingly.

You might decide to structure your day differently to help you manage your stress better. Or, you might practice some anger management techniques before you encounter circumstances that you usually find distressing so you can lengthen your fuse - meaning that a single frustrating episode won't set you off.

Determine if Your Anger Is a Friend or Enemy

Before you spring into action calming yourself down, ask yourself if your anger is a friend or an enemy. If you're witnessing someone's rights being violated or your anger is signaling to you that the circumstances you're in aren't healthy, your anger might be helpful. Then, you might proceed by changing the situation - rather than changing your emotional state. Your anger might give you the courage you need to take a stand or make a change. If, however, your anger is causing distress or it's threatening to cause you to lash out, your anger may be an enemy. In that case, it makes sense to work on changing your emotions by calming yourself down.

Recognize Your Warning Signs

It may feel like your anger hits you in an instant. But, there are warning signs when your anger is on the rise. Recognizing those warning signs can help you take action so you can calm yourself down and prevent your anger from getting to a boiling point.

Think about the physical warning signs of anger. Perhaps your heart beats fast or your face feels hot. Or, maybe you begin to clench your fists. You also might notice some cognitive changes. Perhaps your mind races or you begin "seeing red."

When you recognize your warning signs, you have the opportunity to take immediate action so you can prevent yourself from doing or saying things that create even bigger problems in your life.

Step Away From the Situation

Trying to win an argument or sticking it out in an unhealthy situation will fuel your anger. One of the best things you can do when your anger is on the rise is to take a break. Take a break when a conversation gets heated. Leave a meeting if you think you're going to explode. A time out can be key to helping you calm your brain and your body down.

If there's someone that you routinely get into heated disputes with, like a friend or family member, talk about taking a time-out and resume when you're both feeling calm. Explain that you aren't trying to dodge difficult subjects, but you're working on managing your anger better. And you won't be able to have a productive conversation when you're feeling really upset. You can rejoin the discussion or address the issue again when you're feeling calmer.

Deep Breathing

Deep breathing is important for getting your anger under control. However, taking deep breaths alone is often not enough. Trying to clear your mind and breathe deeply may seem like such a challenge that it only makes your anger and frustration worse.

One of the things that you can do to combat this is to do a little imagining with your deep breathing. Instead of breathing deeply to try to force away your anger, breathe into your anger. Imagine that your anger is this driving energy, and as you breathe deeply it gets bigger and bigger. The energy continues to expand until it is far outside of you, and then it can melt away. This might make you feel angrier at first, but it may work to dispel your anger within a few minutes. Count from 1 to 10 and the urge to yell your lungs out will be gone. You will be able to state your point better.

Change the Way You Think

Angry thoughts add fuel to your anger. Thinking things like, "I can't stand it. This traffic jam is going to ruin everything," will increase your frustration. When you find yourself thinking about things that fuel your anger, reframe your thoughts. Remind yourself of the facts by saying something like, "There are millions of cars on the road every day. Sometimes, there will be traffic jams."

Focusing on the facts - without adding in catastrophic predictions or distorted exaggerations—can help you stay calmer. You also might develop a mantra that you can repeat to drown out the thoughts that fuel your anger. Saying, "I'm OK. Stay calm," or "Not helpful," over and over again can help you keep the thoughts that fuel your anger at bay.

Change the Channel

Ruminating about an upsetting situation fuels angry feelings. If, for example, you've had a bad day at work, rehashing everything that went wrong all evening will keep you stuck in a state of frustration. The best way to calm down might be to change the channel in your brain and focus on something else altogether.

But, you're likely to find that telling yourself "Don't think about that," isn't a good way to get your mind off something. The best way to mentally shift gears is to distract yourself with an activity.

Clean the kitchen, weed the garden, pay some bills, or play with the kids. Find something to do that will keep your mind occupied enough that you won't ruminate on the things upsetting you. Then, your body and your brain can calm down.

Engage in a Relaxation Exercise

There are many different relaxation exercises and it's important to find the one that works best for you. Breathing exercises and progressive muscle relaxation are two common strategies for reducing tension. The best part is, both exercises can be performed quickly and discreetly. So whether you're frustrated at work or you're angry at a dinner engagement, you can let go of stress quickly.

It's important to note, however, that relaxation exercises take practice. At first, you might not feel as though they're effective or you might question whether they're going to work for you. But with practice, they can become your go-to strategies for anger management.

Of course, it is not always possible to exercise when you get angry. However, if you have anger building throughout the day, you can hit the gym after work and get rid of that energy. Taking a walk or going for a run is another form of exercise that you can do to release angry energy. Sometimes if you are in a situation that is making you angry, you can leave that situation and just go for a walk around the block.

Exercising helps your body release the 'feel good' hormone. It will also reduce your stress level, which can be a big reason for being irritable and having anger outburst.

Visualization

If you can separate yourself from the source of your anger for a few minutes, visualization can be helpful in calming yourself and releasing your anger. It is important that you do not visualize harming anyone in this process. Instead, visualize other representations of your anger.

For example, you could visualize an angry tornado ripping through a field, tearing up trees and stirring up dust. Your anger is the tornado, and visualizing this harmless destruction can help you release that anger. After a couple of minutes of the visualization, imagine that the tornado dissipates, along with your anger.

Explore the Feelings Beneath Your Anger

Sometimes it helps to take a moment and think about what emotions might be lurking beneath your anger. Anger often serves as a protective mask to help you avoid feeling more painful emotions, like embarrassment, sadness, and disappointment.

When someone gives you feedback that's hard to hear, for example, you might lash out in anger because you're embarrassed. Convincing yourself the other person is bad for criticizing you might make you feel better by keeping your embarrassment at bay. But, acknowledging those underlying emotions and labeling them can help you get to the root of the problem. Then, you can decide to take appropriate action.

Create a Calm Down Kit

If you tend to come home from work stressed out and you take out your anger on your family or you know that workplace meetings cause you a lot of frustration, create a calm down kit that you can use to relax. Think about objects that might help engage your senses. When you can look, hear, see, smell, and touch calming things, you can change your emotional state.

You might fill a shoebox with scented hand lotion, a photo of you on vacation with your family, a picture of a serene landscape, a spiritual passage about staying calm, and a few pieces of your favorite candy. You might also create a sort of virtual calm down kit that you can take everywhere. Calming music and images, guided meditation, or instructions for breathing exercises could be stored in a special folder on your smartphone.

Send Love And Justice

If a specific person makes you angry, try transforming your anger into thoughts of love and justice. Instead of letting your anger get the best of you in bad traffic, send the driver that has made you angry wishes for getting a ticket or having a near-miss accident that sets him on the straight and narrow. Instead of allowing your anger to control you, transform your anger into thoughts that you wish the best for the person so that they don't make others angry in the future.

Journaling

Journaling can be a great way to release anger. As soon as you can after a situation makes you angry, sit down and write out your thoughts and feelings. Some people find it therapeutic to journal with paper and pen so that it forces them to slow down to articulate their thoughts. Other people find it therapeutic to journal on a computer so that they can bang the keys hard as they type.

The key here is to get all of your thoughts and angry energy and emotions out of you in a healthy and nonviolent way. Journaling allows you to give voice to what you are feeling, which is often the best way to allow yourself to calm down and put those feelings behind you.

Problem Solving

Often, you may become angry because you are frustrated over a situation. Most anger is caused by some kind of problem. If you can change your focus away from the anger to problem-solving, you can diffuse your anger and come up with positive solutions. This is another form of cognitive restructuring. You have to consciously be aware of your thoughts and feelings and stop them in their tracks and change focus to one of solving the problem at hand.

Being angry is never the solution to a problem and can never fix anything. It is important to know what makes you angry and finding ways to alter the situation so that the reason for being angry is gone.

⏺

Take A Time Out

Time outs aren't just for children. When you feel yourself getting angry or irritated and you are worried that you may easily become angry, take a time out. Go to the bathroom and close the door, or go to your car and sit for a few minutes. Even during a workday, there are usually opportunities to take a time out.

When you are in the time out, just focus on your breathing and calming your thoughts. You can use visualization techniques to imagine yourself in a soothing place like a clearing in the woods or your favorite place to go camping. Visualize yourself in nature or some other favorite place. Try to find things in your visualization that engage the senses.

Cognitive Restructuring

Cognitive restructuring is another form of anger management technique that can take some practice but will ultimately serve you well. Cognitive restructuring is all about changing the way you think. It requires you to be mindful of your thoughts and replace angry or uncontrolled thoughts with more positive thoughts.

How you talk to yourself is every bit as important as how you talk to others, perhaps more so. When you tell yourself negative things like "everything is ruined" you are perpetuating a negative emotion. When you change your thinking to tell yourself "this is upsetting and it's understandable to be angry but now it's time to find solutions" you turn that negative energy into something positive.

Cognitive restructuring is not always possible on your own. You may need to get help with this important tool. Studies have shown that cognitive behavioral techniques such as these are among the most effective of anger management techniques. The easiest way to learn these techniques is to go through cognitive behavioral therapy with a therapist.

Using Humor

Humor is a great way to diffuse anger. When you can find the humor in a situation and laugh about it, you will find that your anger is instantly released. It is important that you do not make a situation worse by laughing at someone out of hand. You should also avoid sarcasm, as this can perpetuate an argument and hurt the feelings of others. However, if you can think of something funny about the situation and give voice to it in a positive way you may be able to diffuse not only your own anger but the anger of the person you are arguing with.

Changing Your Environment

One of the things you can immediately do when you are feeling yourself getting angry or frustrated is change your environment. Sometimes escaping the situation is the best thing that you can do. This may require you to leave the room or office for a short period of time. Think of this as kind of a timeout, but for a longer period of time.

You can also change your environment in a lasting way that will help you manage your anger. For example, if you are frequently losing your temper because your child does not clean their room, make sure that the door stays shut so that you don't have to look at it. Since seeing it makes you angry, this small change in your environment can help you prevent that anger.

Talk to a Trusted Friend

If there's someone who has a calming effect on you, talking through an issue or expressing your feelings to that person may be helpful. It's important to note, however, that venting can backfire. Complaining about your boss, describing all the reasons you don't like someone or grumbling about all of your perceived injustices may add fuel to the fire.

A common misconception is that you have to vent your anger to feel better. But, studies show you don't need to "get your anger out." Smashing things when you're upset, for example, may actually make you angrier. So it's important to use this coping skill with caution. If you're going to talk to a friend, make sure you're working on developing a solution or reducing your anger, not just venting. You might find that the best way to use this strategy is to talk about something other than the situation causing you to feel angry.

Try Ayurvedic Remedies

According to the ancient Indian medicine of Ayurveda, an excess of pitta (a type of energy) in the body causes anger (krodha) and anxiety. A variety of cooling herbs such as ashwagandha, brahmi, and basil (tulsi) can balance the pitta energy and calm the nervous system, thereby aiding you in managing your anger and stress more effectively.

Consuming ashwagandha root extract has been scientifically proven to reduce anxiety, stress and lower cortisol levels. Ashwagandha extract is readily available in the form of both herbal tea and dietary supplement capsules. Do remember to consult an experienced Ayurvedic practitioner so you get the dosage right. Basil (tulsi) is also an effective adaptogenic and antidepressant herb that can address psychological stress. Tulsi tea is a great herbal tea to sip once or twice a day. Incorporate into your daily routine and give your immunity a boost as well.

Another effective herbal remedy to lower stress and anxiety (and thereby anger) is brahmi oil. Brahmi oil has been traditionally used to calm the nervous system, lower anxiety, and treat insomnia. A gentle scalp massage using brahmi oil mixed with a little coconut oil can help relax you and lower your stress levels.

Seek Professional Help

Consider anger management counseling if you see that your anger is getting out of control and ruining your relationships. A qualified therapist will be able to help you pinpoint the causes of your anger, understand how to manage it, and channel it in positive ways.

It goes without saying that not all of these techniques are going to work for everyone. Each person is different, with different triggers for their anger, so some of these strategies might be more effective than others. Remember that the point is never to eliminate anger, but to manage it in a manner that minimizes your frustration and unhappiness.

⬚

CHAPTER 6: AWARENESS

Self-awareness involves monitoring our inner worlds, thoughts, emotions, and beliefs. It is important because it's a major mechanism influencing personal development. After spending time researching and writing this book, I've learned that our lives can get out-of-control pretty fast if we are unaware of how and under what circumstances our emotional nature is triggered (for example, we might not realize how much social media upset us).

Self-awareness is a vital first step in taking control of your life, creating what you want, and mastering your future. Where you choose to focus your energy, emotions, personality, and reactions determines where you will end up in life. When you are self-aware, you can see where your thoughts and emotions are guiding you. It also allows you to take control of your actions so you can make the necessary changes to get the outcomes you desire.

This can help if:

• You want to know more about yourself

• You want to develop good self-esteem

• You don't understand other people's reactions to stuff that you're doing.

How Do You Increase Self-Awareness?

Self-awareness requires self-examination. Be aware, though, that an honest, non-judgmental self-analysis isn't easy. We tend to berate ourselves for our failings or fantasize about how great we are when neither is actually the case. We all have a unique mix of "good" and "bad" traits, but we are largely unaware of them. In order to self-reflect objectively, we need to quiet our minds and open our hearts, forgiving ourselves for our imperfections and offering ourselves kudos, but only where we deserve them.

Increasing self-awareness of false attitudes or inappropriate behaviors requires peace of mind, time, attention and focus. Knowing ahead of time that we can indeed change in positive ways through deeper self-awareness makes it worth working on those personal qualities we most value. But first, we must look within ourselves through self-examination to see what's there, which is often less obvious than we think.

Why Does Self-Awareness Matter?

High self-awareness is a solid predictor of good success in life, perhaps because a self-aware person knows when an opportunity is a good fit for them and how to make an appropriate enterprise work well. Quite frankly, most of us are running on "autopilot," hardly aware of why we succeed or fail, or why we behave as we do. Our minds are so busy with daily chatter that we usually only self-reflect when something goes awfully wrong.

Perhaps we stumble through a job interview or academic test we thought we were well prepared for, or we handle something in our lives awkwardly that we assumed we were good at, or perhaps we lose a romantic partner over some misunderstanding where feelings got hurt.

Our response in challenging situations is often to get defensive, make excuses, or blame another person because we don't want to see our own part in the disaster. If we can observe ourselves during such incidents, it will be a good start to self-awareness.

How Do You Build Self-Awareness?

Here are some suggestions to start building self-awareness:

Tune into your feelings - This can be hard if you're not the kind of person who likes to think too deeply about your feelings. Your feelings are spontaneous and emotional responses to the things you experience. Like your senses, they give you good information about what's going on around you, should you choose to tune into them. There are some physical signs that you can look for that might help you to 'read' your feelings. They include:

•   A warm feeling in your face might mean you're embarrassed.

•   A feeling of 'butterflies' in your tummy can mean you're nervous.

- Clenching your teeth might mean you're angry.

In practice: Be aware of physical signs that might indicate how you're feeling. By engaging with how you're feeling, you can get better insights into what you like, what makes you feel uncomfortable and what makes you angry.

Walking, especially in the quiet of nature, can be useful in building self-awareness - The mind tends to wander along with our feet, so with a little conscious nudging (and walking), we can examine our part in something that is happening in our lives now - at work, in social situations, in our relationships, or within the family.

Practicing mindfulness can increase self-awareness - Mindfulness is similar to self-awareness in that they both relate to consciously directing our thoughts inward in order to become more aware of our inner state of being, to observe our thoughts and beliefs, and to notice what triggers our emotions as they rise and fall. Mindfulness includes focused attention in the moment to whatever one is doing and involves practices such as meditation or a quieting of the mind.

Becoming a good listener can increase self-awareness - "Getting out of ourselves" by focusing on another person is a good antidote to stop downward spirals of self-destructive thinking. By being open to someone else, we can learn to listen objectively, even lovingly, to what that person wants to or needs to share. This, in turn, helps teach us how to listen to our own inner dialogues and opinions objectively and lovingly as well.

Becoming more self-aware can be quite enlightening - There is so much we don't know about our inner thoughts and processes that the inward journey at times can be surprising. Sometimes certain phrases come out automatically to reveal attitudes or opinions that we don't even realize we subscribe to or even know where they came from. Over the years of being submerged in a family, a school, various jobs, and a social milieu, we absorb prevailing ideas from our environment, and some of these get buried in our subconscious, where they often don't get examined until we inadvertently blurt them out, at times to our own embarrassment. This is one good reason why it behooves us to become more self-aware . . . to learn how to be ourselves, and to feel more confident that the ideas we are expressing are really our own.

Self-awareness can open your mind to new perspectives - We each tend to have different perspectives on a variety of topics, but as we develop these perspectives, we get comfortable with them and have a preference for our own opinions. However, limited perspectives lead to limited thinking, so by being open to the views of others, we can expand our perspectives to be more universally inclusive. New ideas are refreshing and stimulating, opening our thinking in new and possibly promising directions. Open-mindedness is definitely a plus in being successful at dealing with life's challenges and diverse situations.

Self-awareness is connected to self-esteem - Very often the opinion we hold of ourselves is based on what others think, or more correctly, on what we think others think about us. If we were criticized often as children, we may develop a case of low self-esteem and sensitivity to rejection as a result. On the other hand, if we were praised as a "prince or princess," we are likely to develop high self-esteem, whether deserved or not. So much of our beliefs are buried in the subconscious, where they can do irreparable harm if not examined and re-calibrated to more correctly reflect who we really are.

We owe it to ourselves to become more self-aware of the thoughts and beliefs within. The subconscious holds these ideas and beliefs to be true, so if not examined, we could become a mere sponge for the societal popular mindset and lose much of our uniqueness. Self-awareness can improve our self-esteem because we will know who we are and what we believe, which empowers us to move forward through life with a strong rudder to guide us along our chosen path.

Self-awareness can help you look at yourself objectively - Humans tend to be critical beings, whether self-critical or hard on others, and sometimes both. By beating ourselves up, we serve no one and harm our well-being. And since no one is perfect, why should we expect ourselves to be? So learn to cut through the hype and become more objective, especially about yourself. Yes, there will always be areas where we can improve, but that won't happen if we refuse to take the extra time to develop self-awareness.

When you are alone with your thoughts, there's no reason to take sides. Simply be willing to evaluate yourself as objectively as possible. Be sure not to gloss over what you'd rather not see, but rather mine the subconscious for its opinions and correct the mindsets that are not compatible with your values. You can do this by being completely honest with yourself, and when you find something that is out-of-sync, examine that position, remove what isn't personally compatible, and insert a better value or phrase to bring the idea in alignment with your core values. Do it like you are a teacher correcting a student - not with disdain, but with understanding and compassion. For an extra boost, turn the rephrased concept into an affirmation, and repeat it to yourself as often as necessary to affect the desired change within.

Journaling is a good way to become more self-aware - By writing your thoughts or stream-of-consciousness ideas, you begin opening up to those vulnerable places within. It is here that the mother lode of self-awareness dwells. Journaling isn't everybody's cup of tea, but if you like to write, try it out.

Writing sometimes reveals what contemplation does not, so this method of self-exploration may assist you in expanding your self-awareness. Telling your story, releasing your woes on paper, dreaming up your fantasy situation - these are ways your subconscious can speak to you, revealing what's really "the matter." Let your mind be free and marvel at what it may reveal about you and some of your buried wounds that are crying out for healing. Work with some of these ideas to explore what's behind them with the intention of knowing yourself more intimately.

Feedback from others can help you be more self-aware - Since we are our own best audience, we may miss something in our self-appraisal. That's where the objectivity of others can be most helpful in self-assessment. If you have the courage, ask a friend or acquaintance their opinion of you, or ask about how you managed some project you worked on together or how you handled yourself in some quirky situation.

Constructive criticism is best, of course, but try to be resilient and willing to hear what they have to say. Communication in relationships is extremely important, but you must be open to listening to each other, even when what is said is said imperfectly or is hard to hear. When some aspect of self is revealed that could use some additional refinement, be willing to look behind the obvious to its underlying secret or wound. When you find something that needs some re-tweaking, make a mental or written note to yourself to look at it later when you have some time alone for your self-care.

If, on further examination, a criticism does not appear to be true, consider if they are projecting onto you what they themselves are "guilty" of or struggle with. Perhaps that person is holding a grudge. If so, practice listening to what they have to say and rather than responding defensively, try to get to the bottom of the issue so you can assure a healthy friendship.

Self-awareness can help you know your strengths and weaknesses - "I'm a good starter, but I have more difficulty finishing a project." "It's easy for me to meet new people, but I have reservations when it comes to commitment." "I'm a great friend, but I'm not so good at saving money." We all have strengths and weaknesses, preferences and aversions, and whatever they are, just be aware of them so you don't put yourself in situations where you are unlikely to succeed. Use your strengths to succeed in life, and your path will be happier because you will find appreciation and support along the way.

Self-awareness can help you set intentions - If we wander through life without purpose or direction, chances are we will end up nowhere in particular. In order to form an intention, you really need some idea about what is important to you and what you hope to accomplish. It's not necessary to know how you are going to get there, but you must have some idea of your general direction.

Say your intention out loud and proud, remembering that you are speaking to your inner self, your subconscious, perhaps your higher consciousness, or possibly even to some higher power of your choosing to let them, and you know that you are focused on a certain direction or destination. Use these ideas to communicate with your inner self, letting your subconscious know that you want to better understand your inner mind so that you can live a more meaningful and satisfying life.

?

CHAPTER 7: EMOTIONS! DISCOVER HOW FORGIVE

Sometimes when we are angry we may initially feel as though we cannot forgive the person who has made us angry, especially if the anger has arisen from an issue that is extremely personal.In some respects it is important to learn to forgive people, not purely with regard to religious beliefs but also as a way of setting yourself free from the stress and physical dangers that anger may bring.

Who hasn't been hurt by the actions or words of another? Perhaps a parent constantly criticized you growing up, a colleague sabotaged a project or your partner had an affair. Or maybe you've had a traumatic experience, such as being physically or emotionally abused by someone close to you.

These wounds can leave you with lasting feelings of anger and bitterness - even vengeance. But if you don't practice forgiveness, you might be the one who pays most dearly. By embracing forgiveness, you can also embrace peace, hope, gratitude, and joy. Consider how forgiveness can lead you down the path of physical, emotional and spiritual well-being.

Forgiving those who have hurt you isn't always the easiest thing to do. However, when you learn to forgive others, you are releasing yourself from the anger and negativity that binds you to that person. Forgiveness can help you release deep feelings of sadness and resentment. It can also help you move past negative thoughts that often contribute to anxiety and depression. You deserve to be free of the pain caused by someone else. Learn to let go and accept the past as it was and embrace your life as it is today.

Why You Should Forgive

For many reasons, you may feel that it is too difficult to forgive others who have deeply hurt you. You may feel that the person isn't worthy of your forgiveness. Maybe you fear that forgiving someone will make it appear that you are excusing his or her wrongful actions.

Forgiving someone is not something that comes very easily or very naturally to some people. In order to be able to forgive we must first be able to manage our anger effectively and learn how to release it. Obviously there are ideal ways of doing this including making sure that by releasing our anger we do not harm anyone or cause further and unnecessary problems for anybody else.The term forgiveness when it relates to a negative situation in which someone has harmed or upset you enough to make you angry refers to being able to forgive yourself and understand that you were not part of the problem and didn't deserve the consequential emotions that you have been experiencing. Anger is not necessarily a bad emotion to experience, but when it is allowed to build-up and escalate it hurts you more than anyone else and understanding this can start the process of forgiveness.

Forgiveness can be especially difficult when you never receive an apology that you rightfully deserve. It is certainly possible that the person who wronged you isn't even sorry for what they did. In other circumstances, the person you need to forgive may have passed away, which can make closure even more difficult.

Considering all of these challenges, you may be asking why should you forgive.

For one thing, forgiveness sets us free. When we hold onto the anger, hurt, and resentment associated with what another person did to us, then we are still allowing them to cause damage in our lives. The person may be long gone from your life, but the anger you feel inside still remains. Years will pass by and you will still be holding onto these negative feelings. Forgiveness can be an empowering way to let go of the pain that the other person caused. It is not about excusing a person for cruel or insensitive behavior. Rather, forgiveness is about striving to live your healthiest life and moving past the upsetting actions of others.

Through forgiveness, you can experience other emotional benefits, including improved relationships with those currently in your life. Consider how your deeply held anger and resentment can be affecting your relationships. You may find that when you forgive others that you are more open to trust, love, and acceptance in your current relationships.

Forgiveness also relieves stress, anger, and resentment - feelings that are known to negatively affect the body and mind. Research has determined that managing stress and anger can aid in sleep, reduce anxiety, and improve overall health and wellbeing. Generally, forgiveness provides an opportunity for great personal growth and opens you up to richer and more fulfilling relationships.

Ways to Practice Forgiveness

First of all try and ask yourself whether your problems with anger stem from the actions of other people or a specific other person were meant to be harmful to you and incite anger as most of the time this is not so.If someone has made you angry it can be helpful to remind your self that you are the better person and will not rise to being baited by others who may be trying to goad you into becoming angry.If your anger has stemmed from an event in your past, you may be at risk of carrying this weight around for the rest of your life and may end up endangering your health or feeling increasingly bitter. It is possible to forgive the person who has wronged you even though you may have felt able to do this at first. Releasing your emotions and reflecting on the incident can be very therapeutic and allow you to free yourself of all the stress that has burdened you for so long.

In some respects the art of forgiveness must fall naturally into it's place in the cycle of events. Prematurely pushing yourself into forgiving someone can lead to other effects such as feeling low self-esteem, feeling weak or feeling inadequate as a valued human being. Some people feel guilty when they start feeling forgiving and this can stir up further feelings of anger and we judge ourselves because of it. It shouldn't be rushed, but with the help of family and friends or other outside parties may be achievable at the right time and under the right circumstances and will definitely benefit you and become a valuable part of your anger management. Forgiveness plays a major role in anger management programmes and acceptance of situations and yourself is something that may come naturally but can be assisted by support from either counsellors, therapists or even family and friends.

If you feel ready to forgive, you may be wondering where to start. It is important to keep in mind that forgiveness is a process that can take time and effort to accomplish. I suggest starting small. For example, try to first start forgiving those that only commit minor offenses, such as someone who cuts you off in traffic. Taking such small steps can begin to open your heart to greater acts of forgiveness

Listed here are a few ways to get you started towards forgiving others. Try these activities and see if they can help you on your journey towards forgiveness.

Understand forgiveness - Before you attempt to force forgiveness on your most tender hurts, consider what it is you're asking of yourself: Forgiving doesn't mean that you condone what happened or that the perpetrator is blameless. It is making the conscious choice to release yourself from the burden, pain, and stress of holding on to resentment.

Forgiving doesn't mean that you condone what happened or that the perpetrator is blameless. It is making the conscious choice to release yourself from the burden, pain, and stress of holding on to resentment.

Feel your pain - Hurts can run deep, even if at first glance they don't seem to make a big impact. It's important to give yourself permission to acknowledge and honor the pain that's very real for you. Notice where you feel it in your body and ask yourself, "What do I need right now?" Maybe you need to feel supported, take more time, or do something kind for yourself. Allowing space for the pain in this way can help you know whether you're ready to release it from your heart and mind.

Name it - Whether you've hurt yourself or have been hurt by another, allow yourself to be honest and simply name the feelings that are there. They might include guilt, grief, shame, sorrow, confusion, or anger. As you consider the act of forgiveness, any of these feelings can arise. A study at UCLA found that when you name your emotional experience it turns the volume down on your amygdala, the emotion center of the brain, and brings resources back to your pre-frontal cortex, the rational part of your brain. So, by naming the feeling you can create space and not get overwhelmed.

Let it out - Keeping hurt feelings bottled up only causes additional stress to your mind and body. Even if the memory is difficult to confront, see if you can share how you're feeling. You can write about it in a journal or talk about it with a friend or a professional counselor. Sharing helps you expand your perspective, and perhaps even see what happened through a different lens.

Flip your focus - If possible, see if you can flip your focus from being the victim to putting yourself in the other person's shoes. For example, consider the life the person lived that led them to this hurtful action. This is difficult to do, but remember, you're not condoning any action. This exercise is just about trying to see that, as humans, we are deeply impacted by our own traumas and life experiences, which greatly inform how we show up and act in the world. If you are able to do this, compassion naturally tends to flow from this more understanding perspective.

Take action - Whether you are forgiving yourself or another person, taking action can help to facilitate healing and make you feel more empowered. It's best to start with smaller misdeeds to get into practice and feel what's possible. Writing a letter or having an uncomfortable conversation can be difficult and even scary, but often a sense of empowerment emerges from the self-compassionate action of listening to yourself and doing something that supports you.

Remember, you're not the first or last - When you've been hurt, it's common to feel like you're the only one who has ever been wronged in this way. In fact, it's likely that this transgression (or something similar to it) has been made many, maybe even millions of times before throughout human history. Making mistakes is part of our shared human experience. Remembering you are not alone in experiencing this kind of pain can help to loosen your grip on your resentment.

Have patience; forgiveness is a practice - Forgiveness isn't a quick-fix solution. It's a process, so be patient with yourself. With smaller transgressions, forgiveness can happen pretty quickly, but with the larger ones, it can take years. As you begin with the smaller misdeeds and then move onto the harder ones, be kind to yourself, take deep breaths, and continue on.

Stop blaming - We all know it can feel good now and again to complain to a friend - misery loves company, right? Well, not exactly. Blaming is a way to discharge pain and discomfort. It gives us a false sense of control but inevitably keeps the negativity kicking around in our minds, increasing our stress and eroding our relationships.

Practice more mindfulness - A recent study surveyed 94 adults who had been cheated on by their partners and found a correlation between traits of mindfulness and forgiveness. In other words, it can be said that the more you practice mindfulness, the more you strengthen your capacity for forgiveness.

Find meaning and strength through your pain - As you practice working with the pain that's there, you grow key strengths of self-compassion, courage, and empathy that inevitably make you stronger in every way. As psychiatrist and Holocaust survivor Viktor Frankl wrote in Man's Search for Meaning, even in the most horrific and painful circumstances, we have the freedom to create meaning in life, which is a powerful healing agent.

You understandably have many feelings of anger toward the person who hurt you. Get these feelings out by writing the person a letter. Let them know in detail all the ways in which they hurt you and how you have felt about it. Get as honest as possible, releasing all of your pent up emotions onto paper. Let the person know that you have decided to forgive them. You can even explain why you are forgiving, such as writing, "I forgive you because I no longer want to hold on to the pain you have caused." Once your letter is complete rip up into shreds. This activity will allow you to release emotions that needed to be expressed and then let them go.

A Mini Forgiveness Practice:

Try this short practice once a day and feel your forgiveness muscles growing. Think of someone who has caused you pain (to start, maybe not the person who has hurt you most) and you're holding a grudge against. Visualize the time you were hurt by this person and feel the pain you still carry. Hold tightly to your unwillingness to forgive. Now, observe what emotion is present. Is it anger, resentment, sadness?

Use your body as a barometer and notice physically what you feel. Are you tense anywhere, or do you feel heavy? Next, bring awareness to your thoughts; are they hateful, spiteful, or something else?

Really feel this burden associated with the hurt that lives inside you, and ask yourself: "Who is suffering? Have I carried this burden long enough? Am I willing to forgive?"

If the answer is no, that's OK. Some wounds need more time than others to heal. If you are ready to let it go now, silently repeat: "Breathing in, I acknowledge the pain. Breathing out, I am forgiving and releasing this burden from my heart and mind."

Continue this process for as long as it feels supportive to you.

⟨?⟩

CHAPTER 8: ANGER MANAGEMENT CLASSES

Anger management classes may have been recommended by a doctor or mental health professional or may even be part of a legal process and condition of release from custody, but it is not only these people who might benefit from the exert advice and guidance offered by these service providers.

Anger management classes are sessions that aim to help those who are struggling to deal with their anger effectively. These people may be extremely troubled by their problems and might be using anger as a way of masking their past, as a means of disguising how they are coping in general or simply to help those who feel that their anger has or is about to cause them to become violent. The sessions are usually run by professionals, including doctors and therapists who have been trained in the subject area and have methods and techniques that they can teach that the individual can learn and use when they feel their anger level is rising. They can also be useful for helping people understand how and why their anger has developed to such extremes; often this may mean the person has to face issues that are highly emotional and learning how to address these in a less aggressive, or more productive and understanding way. The environment aims to offer support and guidance for the client and works closely with people as individuals assessing each case very carefully, making their work client-centered.

Self-Referring To Anger Management Classes

These classes are most frequently used by those who have used violence as a way of expressing their anger and these people will take preference over non-violent clients in most cases. If you would like to attend anger management classes you might want to start by asking your doctor of any local groups or whether they could ask a mental health professional for a recommended group. An Internet search may provide plenty of results which allows for careful research of each provider. The types of issues that could be considered are the location of the group, the times at which it is available, and the costs of the session, whether they run single sessions or a course of treatment and the type of theory or model that is used. Most anger management classes will encourage the client to learn how to communicate more effectively, how to express themselves without violence or aggression and how to remain calm in stressful or tense situations. Many sessions will also teach clients how to become more self-aware and equip them with tools that can be relied upon when an anger outburst would previously have been the norm.

Anger management session are most often run by trained professionals who have either a counselling, psychology or therapeutic background and specialize in the field of anger management. Always make sure you have researched your provider if you have self-referred as there are few legal requirement that prevent anyone from setting up their own business as an anger management specialist.

What Will I Have To Do?

If you are struggling very badly with your anger and pose a threat to those around you may be offered a one-to-one intensive session. If you have booked a session you must attend unless an emergency prevents you from doing so. You have taken the first step to decreasing your anger and controlling your responses by booking on the course so it would be unproductive to not follow it through. For those who have been told they must attend as a legal requirement the consequences of not attending may be very detrimental to your case. You should follow the session or program to the end when you will probably have to re-assess you current feelings and responses to stimuli using the techniques offered during the sessions. If you have self-referred you may incur some costs and these can be quite expensive so it may be worth asking your GP or local social services department if you are entitled to receive any help with these costs.

Anger management classes are very effective for helping people deal with their repressed feelings and coping strategies if they are not dealing with anger very well or are increasingly experiencing it. They may be funded for you or will incur a private cost.

The Costs

The costs for anger management classes are very varied and may depend on the location of the class, the expertise of the providers, the length of the course, any materials needed and whether you will receive any follow-up care.

Anger management classes are extremely beneficial for those who feel their anger is getting on top of them or they are ready to explode. If you are feeling increasingly angry and your work and home life and affected, or someone has advised you that you may benefit from anger management it is recommended that this course of therapy is explored before anger causes you to seriously compromise yourself or damage your health.

⁂

CHAPTER 9: GET OUT THE STRESS FROM YOUR LIFE

It seems like you hear it all the time from nearly everyone you know - "I'm SO stressed out!" Pressures abound in this world today. Those pressures cause stress and anxiety, and often we are ill-equipped to deal with those stressors that trigger anxiety and other feelings that can make us sick. Literally, sick.

The statistics are staggering. One in every eight Americans age 18-54 suffers from an anxiety disorder. This totals over 19 million people! Research conducted by the National Institute of Mental Health has shown that anxiety disorders are the number one mental health problem among American women and are second only to alcohol and drug abuse by men.

Women suffer from anxiety and stress almost twice as much as men. Anxiety disorders are the most common mental illness in America, surpassing even depression in numbers. Anxiety is the most common mental health issue facing adults over 65 years of age. Anxiety disorders cost the U.S. $46.6 billion annually. Anxiety sufferers see an average of five doctors before being successfully diagnosed. Unfortunately, stress and anxiety go hand in hand. In fact, one of the major symptoms of stress is anxiety. And stress accounts for 80 percent of all illnesses either directly or indirectly.

In fact, stress is more dangerous than we thought. You've probably heard that it can raise your blood pressure, increasing the likelihood of a stroke in the distant future, but recently a health insurance brochure claimed that 90 percent of visits to a primary care physician were stress-related disorders. Health Psychology magazine reports that chronic stress can interfere with the normal function of the body's immune system. And studies have proven that stressed individuals have an increased vulnerability to catching an illness and are more susceptible to allergic, autoimmune, or cardiovascular diseases.

Doctors agree that during chronic stress, the functions of the body that are nonessential to survival, such as the digestive and immune systems, shut down. This is why people get sick. There are also many occurrences of psychosomatic illness, an illness with an emotional or psychological side to it.

Furthermore, stress often prompts people to respond in unhealthy ways such as smoking, drinking alcohol, eating poorly, or becoming physically inactive. This damages the body in addition to the wear and tear of the stress itself. Stress is a part of daily life. It's how we react to it that makes all the difference in maintaining our health and well-being. Pressures occur throughout life and those pressures cause stress. You need to realize that you will never completely get rid of stress in your life, but you can learn coping techniques to turn that stress into a healthier situation.

Why Are You So Stressed Out?

We're living in very trying and difficult times and things don't seem to be getting any easier. Sometimes life can seem terribly painful and unfair, yet somehow we manage to struggle on, day after day, hoping and praying that things will soon get better. But day by day the world is becoming a crazier and more uncertain place to live in, not to mention stressful. Nothing seems safe anymore. Millions of people are in record levels of debt. Many are losing their jobs, their homes, their health and sometimes even their sanity. Worry, depression, and anxiety seem to have become a way of life for way too many people. We seem to have entered the Age of Anxiety. In fact, in 2012, the cover of Time magazine proclaimed this loud and clear on one of their covers as the featured story in that issue. The constant stress and uncertainties of living in the 21st century have certainly taken their toll, and as a result, many of us seem to live a life of constant fear and worry. When the terrorist attacks happened on September 11, this constant stress and worry seemed to just be magnified. In fact, many people even now four years later report they are still scared that something of that magnitude could happen again – perhaps closer to them. Turn on the news or open up a newspaper and we are bombarded with disturbing images and stories. We begin to wonder if we are safe anywhere. In this, the information age, never before have we had so much access to so much data.

The economy is another stressor. Our country is in debt and so are many Americans. Soaring gas prices, outrageous housing costs, even the cost of food has sent many Americans to work in jobs that are unsatisfying and tedious. They work these jobs because they need a paycheck. Today, it's more important to bring home the bacon rather than work in a dream career. Having more women in the workplace adds to the stress. So many women feel the need to be everything to everyone and that includes a paycheck earner, housekeeper, mom, wife, daughter, and sibling. The only problem with that is some women just don't make any time for themselves thus contributing to their stress levels being at an all-time high.

Even children can feel the pressure of stress and anxiety. Teenagers who want to go to college find themselves pushing themselves during their studies to try and obtain scholarships so they can attend schools that have ever increasing tuition costs. They find themselves having to hold down part-time jobs on top of all that to earn money for extras that their parents can no longer afford. Add peer pressure into the mix and you have a veritable pressure cooker! Cell phones, internet, palm pilots, blackberries, I-pods – we are always on the go and always reachable. We don't make time to relax and enjoy life anymore. Why not? We certainly should! We feel pressure to do these things because we think we have to, not because we want to. All too often, it's difficult for people to just say "No". Not saying that one little word piles up un-needed expectations and obligations that make us feel anxious.

All of us will experience situations that may cause us to become stressed or feel anxious. The reasons are too many to note but can include, buying a property, having guests stay over, being bullied, exams, looking after children, managing finances, relationship issues, traveling, etc. Stress is a 'normal' function of everyday life. Only when it appears to take over our lives does it then become a problem. Everyone will have different reasons why a situation causes them pressure. As a rule, it's usually when we don't feel in control of a situation, then we feel its grip tightening around us causing us to feel worried or 'stressed'. If stress is caused by us not feeling in control of a situation, the answer is to try and reverse this and regain that control. The good news is: You Can! You have everything inside you that you need to overcome your stress and the accompanying anxiety. The problem is, often we don't realize that we are in control because we feel so out of control at time. But the tools are there, you just have to use them.

Let's first look at the barriers we put up that are preventing us from becoming healthy and getting rid of our anxiety and stress.

There are three obsessive behaviors that you are likely to be engaging in that impeded your healing process and stop you from enjoying a stress-free life. Recognizing these barriers can be a great first step toward getting rid of the problems that go with being too stressed.

The first is obsessive negativity. When you are obsessively negative, it means that you have a tendency toward being "negative" about people, places, situations, and things in your life.

Perhaps you find yourself saying things like "I can't do this!" or "No one understands!" or "Nothing ever works!", for example. You may be doing this unconsciously, but essentially you have what's known as a "sour grapes" attitude, and it holds you back from knowing what it's like to view life from a positive lens and enjoy the beauty in yourself and people around you! There's a whole world out there for you...with happiness and positive thinking.

Then you have obsessive perfectionism. When you engage in obsessive perfectionism, you are centered on trying to do everything "just so" to the point of driving yourself into an anxious state of being. You may find yourself making statements such as, "I have to do this right, or I'll be a failure!" or "If I am not precise, people will be mad at me!" Again, this behavior may be totally under the threshold of your awareness, but it interferes greatly with your ability to enjoy things without feeling "uptight" and "stressed."

Finally, there is obsessive analysis. When you are obsessed about analyzing things, you find yourself wanting to re-hash a task or an issue over and over again. For instance, you might find yourself making statements such as, "I need to look this over, study it, and know it inside and out...or else I can't relax!" or "If I relax and let things go without looking them over repeatedly, things go wrong!"

While analytical thinking is an excellent trait, if it's done in excess you never get to stop and smell the roses because you're too busy trying to analyze everything and everyone around you. Gaining insight into this type of behavior is one of the most important keys to letting go of stress, and getting complete power over your anxiety. If you find yourself engaging in any of the above "Blocking Behaviors", there are two things you can do to help yourself.

First, ask the people you know, love, and trust, "Am I negative about things?", "Do I complain a lot?", and "Am I difficult to be around?" This may be hard for you to listen to, as the truth sometimes hurts a great deal. But the insight you will get from others' assessment of you is invaluable, and you'll know precisely how others see you. Accept their comments as helpful info, and know that you will gain amazing insights from what you hear.

Second, keep a journal to write down and establish patterns of when you are using "blocking behaviors." Even if you are not thrilled with the idea of writing, you can make little entries into a notebook or journal each day. The great part is that you'll begin to see patterns in your behavior that reveal exactly what you're doing to prevent yourself from curing your anxiety.

Calm Yourself With Visualization

The purpose of visualization is to enable you to quickly clear mental stress, tension, and anxious thinking. The visualization can be used when feeling stressed and is particularly useful when your mind is racing with fearful, anxious thinking.

This visualization process, when practiced frequently, is very effective for eliminating deep-seated mental anxieties or intrusive thoughts. To gain maximum benefit, the exercise must be carried out for longer than 10 minutes at a time, as anything shorter will not bring noticeable results. There is no right or wrong way to carry out the visualization. Be intuitive with it and do not feel you are unable to carry it out if you feel you are not very good at seeing mental imagery. As long as your attention is on the exercise, you will gain benefit. It is best to do this exercise in a quiet place where you won't be disturbed, and then when you are more practiced you will be able to get the same positive results in a busier environment such as the workplace.

You should notice a calming effect on your state of mind along with a sensation of mental release and relaxation. Either sitting or standing, close your eyes and move your attention to your breath. To become aware of your breathing, place one hand on your upper chest and one on your stomach. Take a breath and let your stomach swell forward as you breathe in and fall back gently as you breathe out. Take the same depth of breath each time and try to get a steady rhythm going. Your hand on your chest should have little or no movement. Again, try to take the same depth of breath each time you breathe in. This is called Diaphragmatic Breathing.

When you feel comfortable with this technique, try to slow your breathing rate down by instituting a short pause after you have breathed out and before you breathe in again. Initially, it may feel as though you are not getting enough air in, but with regular practice, this slower rate will soon start to feel comfortable.

It is often helpful to develop a cycle where you count to three when you breathe in, pause, and then count to three when you breathe out (or 2, or 4 - whatever is comfortable for you). This will also help you focus on your breathing without any other thoughts coming into your mind. If you are aware of other thoughts entering your mind, just let them go and bring your attention back to counting and breathing. Continue doing this for a few minutes. (If you practice this, you will begin to strengthen the Diaphragmatic Muscle, and it will start to work normally - leaving you with a nice relaxed feeling all the time.)

Now move your attention to your feet. Try to really feel your feet. See if you can feel each toe. Picture the base of your feet and visualize roots growing slowly out through your soles and down into the earth. The roots are growing with quickening pace and are reaching deep into the soil of the earth. You are now rooted firmly to the earth and feel stable like a large oak or redwood tree.

Stay with this feeling of grounded safety and security for a few moments. Once you have created a strong feeling or impression of being grounded like a tree, visualize a cloud of bright light forming way above you. A bolt of lightning from the luminous cloud hits the crown of your head, and that ignites a band of bright white light descending slowly from your head all the way down your body, over your legs, and out past your toes. As the band of light passes over you, feel it clearing your mental state. It is illuminating your mind and clearing any disturbing or stressful thoughts that you may have been thinking about. Repeat this image four or five times until you feel a sense of clearing and release from any anxious thinking. In finishing, see yourself standing under a large, luminescent waterfall. The water is radiant and bubbling with vitality and life. As you stand under the waterfall, you can feel the water run over every inch of your body, soothing you and instilling within you a sense of deep calm.

Try to taste the water. Open your mouth and let it run into your mouth, refreshing you. Hear it as it bounces off the ground around you. The water is life itself and it is washing away stress and worry from your mind and body. After a moment, open your eyes. Try to use all of your senses when carrying out the visualization. To make the pictures in your mind as real as possible, use your senses of touch, taste, and hearing. Feel the water trickle down your body; hear the sound it makes as it splashes over you. The more realistic the imagined scenarios, the more benefit you will gain.

Many people report very beneficial and soothing results from using these simple visualizations frequently. The mind is much like a muscle in that, in order to relax, it needs to regularly release what it is holding onto. You can use any situation or location that will help calm you. We liken this to "finding your happy place". Maybe you feel relaxed in a swimming pool or on the beach. Imagine yourself there. Just make sure wherever you go in your mind is a place where you can be calm and rested.

By visualizing the different situations, you are allowing your mind to release. It is like sending a message to your brain that when you close your eyes and begin this process it is time for letting go of anything that it has been mentally holding onto, including anxious thinking. In order to train your mind how to let go of the stress, it is important to practice this daily. With practice, you can learn to release all stress within minutes of starting the exercise. Your daily practice should take place before going to bed, as that will enable you to sleep more soundly.

Many people do not do these visualizations in the bedroom but some other room before going to bed. That way, when they enter the bedroom and close the door, they are leaving the mental stress and anxious thinking behind them. Just be sure you have the opportunity to totally concentrate on your mental images. Visualization as a tool for dealing with mental stress is very effective. If such visualization is carried out properly, you can reach a deep feeling of inner calm. This technique probably will not work in helping to end an anxiety attack, but it can help that attack from beginning. It is a very powerful support tool for ridding yourself of general anxiety sensations.

With practice, you find you go days without having anxious thinking interrupt your life, and importantly, this significantly reduces the level of general anxiety you feel. Visualization is simply a tool you can use to overcome anxious thoughts and feelings. Let's look at various ways that you can combat excessive stress – beginning with music.

Using Music To Beat Stress

Listening to music does wonder to alleviate stress. Everyone has different tastes in music. We should listen to the music that makes us feel comfortable. Sitting down and forcing yourself to listen to relaxation music that you don't like may create stress, not alleviate it.

Music is a significant mood-changer and reliever of stress, working on many levels at once. The entire human energetic system is extremely influenced by sounds, the physical body and chakra centers respond specifically to certain tones and frequencies. Special consideration should be given to the positive effects of one actually playing or creating music themselves. Among the first stress-fighting changes that take place when we hear a tune is an increase in deep breathing. The body's production of serotonin also accelerates.

Playing music in the background while we are working, seemingly unaware of the music itself, has been found to reduce the stress of the workplace. That's why so many retail places play music while you shop – to take your mind off the high prices!

Music was found to reduce heart rates and to promote higher body temperature - an indication of the onset of relaxation. Combining music with relaxation therapy was more effective than doing relaxation therapy alone. Many experts suggest that it is the rhythm of the music or the beat that has the calming effect on us although we may not be very conscious about it. They point out that when we were a baby in our mother's womb, we probably were influenced by the heartbeat of our mother. We respond to the soothing music at later stages in life, perhaps associating it with the safe, relaxing, protective environment provided by our mother. Music can be one of the most soothing or nerve-wracking experiences available.

Choosing what will work for any individual is difficult, most will choose something they 'like' instead of what might be beneficial. In doing extensive research on what any given piece of music produces in the physiological response system many unexpected things were found. Many of the so-called meditation and relaxation recordings actually produced adverse

EEG patterns, just as bad as Hard Rock and Heavy Metal.

The surprising thing was many selections of Celtic, Native American, as well as various music containing loud drums or flute, were extremely soothing. The most profound finding was any music performed live and even at moderately loud volumes even if it was somewhat discordant had very a beneficial response.

As we mentioned before, there is not a single music that is good for everyone. People have different tastes. It is important that you like the music being played. I recently picked up a rest and relaxation CD at Wal-Mart that has done wonders for me. It has the sounds of the ocean in the background while beautiful piano music plays. It's very soothing. One note here, it's probably not a good idea to play certain types of ballads or songs that remind you of a sad time in your life when you're trying to de-stress. The reason is obvious. You're trying to relax and wash away the anxious thoughts. The last thing that you need is for a sad song to bring back memories you don't need anyway.

Here are some general guidelines to follow when using music to de-stress.

• To wash away stress, try taking a 20-minute "sound bath." Put some relaxing music on your stereo, and then lie in a comfortable position on a couch or on the floor near the speakers. For a deeper experience, you can wear headphones to focus your attention and to avoid distraction.

•   Choose music with a slow rhythm - slower than the natural heartbeat which is about 72 beats per minute. Music that has repeating or cyclical pattern is found to be effective in most people.

•   As the music plays, allow it to wash over you, rinsing off the stress from the day. Focus on your breathing, letting it deepen, slow and become regular. Concentrate on the silence between the notes in the music; this keeps you from analyzing the music and makes relaxation more complete.

•   If you need stimulation after a day of work, go for a faster music rather than slow calming music. Turn up the volume and DANCE! It doesn't matter if you can actually dance or not. Just move along with the music and do what feels good. You'll be shocked at the release you can feel! •When going gets tough, go for a music you are familiar with - such as a childhood favorite or favorite oldies. Familiarity often breeds calmness.

•   Take walks with your favorite music playing on the walkman. Inhale and exhale in tune with the music. Let the music takes you. This is a great stress reliever by combining exercise (brisk walk), imagery and music.

- Listening to the sounds of nature, such as ocean waves or the calm of a deep forest, can reduce stress. Try taking a 15- to 20-minute walk if you're near the seashore or a quiet patch of woods. If not, you can buy tapes of these sounds in many music stores. This has been very calming for me - you should try it too.

There's another great relaxation technique that I have found in coping with my own anxiety problems: self-hypnosis.

Self-Hypnosis For Stress

A few weeks ago, I was feeling particularly overwhelmed with stress and anxiety. It seemed like anything that could go wrong, did go wrong. I felt like I was spinning out of control. I happened to be writing a book on yoga and meditation at the time and came across a website that offered a downloadable MP3 hypnotic relaxation session. It cost me about $20 and it was the best $20 I have ever spent.

There are plenty of places on the internet where you can get these downloadable sessions for a small fee. However, you can also practice self-hypnosis on your own. You first need to find a quiet place where you can fully relax and listen to your inner voice. You shouldn't try to make something happen. Let your mind listen and relax.

A large part of achieving that hypnotic state is to allow it to happen naturally. Also, don't watch for certain signs or signals that you might be in a hypnotic state. We can guarantee that if you look for these signs, you won't be able to fully relax and gain the benefits of self-hypnosis. There are lots of different ways to experience hypnosis. No two people will have exactly the same experience. In one respect, though, everyone has the same experience: the hypnotic state is always pleasant!

There are no "bad trips" in hypnosis. Keep in mind that self-hypnosis is a skill and that you will continue to get better at it and, as you do, it becomes ever more powerful. It's a good idea to set up a schedule of practice, allowing yourself anywhere between 10 and 30 minutes, depending on how busy you are and how much time you have to spend at it. Practice during the best part of your day if you can and at a time when you are least likely to be disturbed by others. Most people find it best to practice lying down, in a comfortable position, with as few distractions as possible. If you are bothered by noise while you practice you can try to mask out the noise with some other source of sound.

You can try stereo music in the background, or white noise if you like. If like most people you don't have a white noise generator, try tuning a radio receiver between stations. The static you get when you do that is similar to white noise. However, this takes an older or cheaper FM receiver without a noise suppressor. Sometimes AM tuners can be used for this. This should just be in the background and not too loud to be distracting.

Channel Anger in a Creative Way

Learning how to direct and channel aggression, rage and anger will enable you to reduce the amount of stressful situations and problems in your life.

Get Positive To help create a positive feeling it is important to release the pressure of anger and aggression. You may be able to do this by taking slow, deep breaths and repeating positive affirmations like 'I am relaxing and doing fine' as your body releases tension. Or you may get the urge to let out the tension in a more audible way, by shouting it out. If this is the case, finding a safe, secluded place in nature, or screaming into a pillow may provide you with a beneficial solution to reducing your feelings of anger. Thinking positively will encourage you to explore different styles of channeling anger, and will keep you motivated to take action.

Get Creative. There are many creative options to explore when looking for effective ways to channel your anger. Listening to soothing music, dancing to favourite tunes or painting all induce a relaxing effect on us. Not only will you be channeling your rage by concentrating your focus on the activity, but you will also be shifting your emotions and feelings so that they become less aggressive and more positively calm. Keeping a Journal will also provide you with an opportunity to explore your creativity. Expressing your deepest feelings in writing well help you clarify why you react in the way that you do in certain situations. It will also help you channel your emotions by shifting your focus to the way you are expressing your thoughts and beliefs.

Get Active. Physical activity not only benefits our body but it also creates a positive response in our mind. Feel-good chemicals are released in the body whenever we exercise or move energetically, so going to the gym, exercising outdoors, dancing and playing with your children can all help us ease feelings of anger and frustration. Quiet contemplation, in the form of yoga, pilates, t'ai chi or meditation can also have a powerful effect on reducing pent-up anger. Because these activities are slower and more precise they require that we focus all of our attention on the exercise in question. Stilling our thoughts, so that we can enjoy this form of creative channeling, will enable us to shift our aggressive emotions and feelings so that they become softer and more manageable.

Get Talkative. If you are fortunate enough to have an understanding friend or family member, talking about your feelings will enable you to express your emotions in a comfortable and safe environment. Being able to calmly express how you feel when anger threatens to overwhelm you, will help you understand why you react to situations, and individuals, in the manner that you do. Accepting your friend's opinion will also enable you to identify the best way to channel any feelings that you may experience in the future.

⁇

CHAPTER 10: KEEP CALM AT EVERY PROVOCATIONS

There's a lot going on in this world. In fact, there's probably a lot going on in your life at the moment. So much to do, so little time, and just too much uncertainty. You probably feel as though you are constantly fighting against the odds while trying to make your way in this world.

As you work through your problems you need to fight through stress, anxiety, fear, anger, frustration, overwhelm and a plethora of other emotions. These emotions leave you in a frantic state, which negatively affects your health and hurts your ability to make good decisions.

The one certainty about life is that it will put you under intense pressure situation. And when emotions get the better of you, you will most likely fail to capitalize on your greatest opportunities moving forward. In fact, your ability to stay calm under provocations could be the difference between the success you desire to create in your life, and complete and utter failure.

Developing the ability to stay calm under provocation situations means that you are less likely to suffer from the effects of stress, anxiety, and worry. Your calm approach will also lead to better health and higher levels of productivity. It will provide you with a sense of control over the events and circumstances of your life, and most certainly a better sense of control over yourself, your thoughts and emotions. On top of this, staying calm under provocations will help improve your ability to focus on the right things, at the right time, and in the right way. It will allow you to better communicate your needs to other people, and help you make more effective, intelligent and emotional-free decisions.

The Qualities of Calmness

In order to reap the rewards that a state of calmness can bring into your life, you will need to become more mindful. Being more mindful means being more centered and focused on the moment. It means letting go of past regrets. It means redirecting your mind away from current stresses, and it also means refocusing yourself away from future worries. It's all about being mindful - being present in the moment - because it's in the moment where you will find the answers you need that will help you solve your life's problems.

A state of calmness also requires patience. Sometimes you need a little patience and time to understand the events and circumstances of your life. Sometimes you need the patience to gain a deeper insight into your predicament. And the only way you will find true and unadulterated patience in a state of calmness.

Likewise, calmness also requires optimism and faith. You need optimism to help you find the motivation you need to journey through the thick dark fog of your provocations. And you need faith to help you find your way when you lose yourself in the turmoil of your emotions. Optimism will help you find the desire you need to move forward, and faith will provide you with the courage you need to persist through the obstacles that stand in your way.

Things to do When Under Provoking Situations

As you go about your day, there will be moments when you will face provoking situations. Something unexpected might happen, your emotions will spin out of control, and it will momentarily seem as though the entire weight of the world has fallen on your shoulders. It's moments like these that a steady hand and calm mind are of utmost importance. In fact, the decision you make at this very moment could either help you improve the situation or might very well make things much worse than they already are.

In order to make the right decision, you will need to stay calm, centered and focused on the right things and in the right way. Here are some suggestions:

Immediately Remove Yourself from the Situation - When under provocation, take time to immediately remove yourself from the situation temporarily. Having removed yourself physically and emotionally from the situation, take time now to clarify why you're feeling pressured. Ask yourself:

•   Why am I suddenly feeling provoked?

•   What has triggered my feelings?

•   What has ruffled my emotions?

•   Has something outside of me triggered my emotions?

•   Am I seeing things clearly?

•   Am I interpreting the situation correctly?

•   Is it possible that my perspective of this situation has triggered my emotions?

Sometimes the things that trigger your emotions are phantoms. You're feeling provoked, but the provocation isn't coming from an external force, but rather from within — from inside you. You are in fact creating the emotional provocation within yourself, and this is causing you to feel provoked externally. This is an illusion. It's a trick your mind is playing on you. It's important you recognize this because changing things might only require a simple shift of perspective on your part.

It's important to gain clarity about what it is you want because unless you a clear about what you want, you will fail to make the right decisions that will help you move through this situation successfully. Moreover, gaining clarity will help you filter out unnecessary and irrelevant factors. It will allow you to re-prioritize the things you need to focus on to help you get through this difficult emotional experience.

Prioritizing things accordingly helps you to focus on the most important and relevant factors that will allow you to move through this situation successfully. In fact, the moment you pinpoint these critical areas is the moment you can begin working your way through this situation in a more intelligent and calming manner. No longer should the circumstances of the situation phase you. Instead, you should now be in full control of your emotional responses, and can now calmly and sensibly work through your problems.

If after going through these sets of questions you are still finding your emotions overwhelming and difficult to deal with, then consider the lighter-side of the situation. Ask yourself:

•   What's funny about this?

Hopefully, the answer to this question will help shift your perspective about your circumstances. It might even help you relax and calm yourself down. And that might be all you need to move through this situation successfully.

Always be Attentive - During the provoking situations, it's absolutely paramount that you pay attention to the details. It's in the details that you will find the answers and the opportunities you need to move forward.

When a situation presents itself, it's natural to immediately become overwhelmed by the circumstances. And because you're overwhelmed, you naturally bundle all your concerns and problems into one big messy pile of puzzle pieces in your head. There is no separation between things. Everything becomes one thing, and this is what overwhelms you.

The better way to handle yourself is to pay attention to the details. Be attentive to the little things, to your behavior, to other people's behavior, to the circumstances and all the external things going on around you. The more attentive you are, the more you will pick-up. And as a result you will no longer bundle everything into one big uncontrollable problem, instead, you will see things as individual pieces that are part of the larger puzzle that you now need to figure out how to solve.

Use Empowering Language - The mindset you bring into provocation is absolutely critical. Part of this mindset is the language you use to talk to yourself during these difficult emotional moments. Your language can either help you calm yourself down, or it can lead you down the path of overwhelm and panic. For instance, saying:

- I can handle this…

- I am in control…

- I am calm…

- I am focused…

This type of language will make you feel centered, calm and in control of yourself and your emotions. And because you're in control of your emotional responses, you will now be able to make better decisions moving forward that will help you to work through this pressure situation far more effectively.

Ask Calming Questions - Another aspect of empowering language is the process of asking the right kinds of questions that will help you to stay calm, centered and focused on the right things. For instance, during pressure situations try asking yourself:

- What's good about this?

- What are the benefits of staying calm?

- How will a calm mind help me work through this situation successfully?

These types of questions will help you maintain control of your emotions. They will also help you to redirect your emotions in a more positive and helpful way.

Avoid Unhelpful Thinking Habits - The language you use and the questions you ask yourself translate into the thoughts you indulge in during provocation situations. These thoughts can either be empowering and helpful, or they can be limiting and unhelpful.

Examples of unhelpful thoughts include blaming yourself, blaming other people, or blaming your circumstances. Unhelpful thoughts can also include over-analyzing the situation and getting lost in too many details; magnifying the negatives of the situation; and/or over-dramatizing events and circumstances in unhelpful ways. All of these methods of thinking about your situation are not helpful. In fact, thinking this way will make you feel absolutely miserable and will prevent you from moving forward in a calm and controlled fashion.

Instead, focus on things you can control. And that control comes from within yourself. You can control the language you use and the questions you ask yourself. Once you have these things under your control, you will likewise gain control over your emotional responses and thoughts. And this will naturally lead to a greater sense of calmness and emotional stability, which is exactly what you need to help you get through this pressure situation successfully.

Guidelines for Finding Ways to Calm Down and Relax

In order to handle provocation situations far more effectively, you will need to become a more relaxed and calm individual. Calmness is, of course, a state-of-mind, however, in order to get to that state-of-mind, you will need to adopt some new habits, behaviors and potentially shake up your routine a little to allow time for more relaxation and periods of self-reflection.

Here are some suggestions to help you find ways to relax and reflect more throughout the day:

Build a Calming Environment - Calmness, of course, begins from within, on a psychological level. However, it's difficult to maintain an inner sense of calmness if your environment is frantic, chaotic and disorganized. As such, it's important to build an environment that will make it easier for you to maintain a calm mental state-of-mind.

Building a relaxing and nurturing working environment depends entirely on what specifically makes you feel comfortable and relaxed. You might like to install some colored lights, play peaceful music, use tranquil nature sounds, stimulate the senses with aromatherapy, or maybe even use a well-placed fountain or some candles to help bring a warm, peaceful and friendly energy into the room. The choice is completely yours to make.

Build a Calming Daily Routine - There may very well be moments of your day that are frantic and hectic. These moments are simply a part of your working life, and it can certainly be difficult to work around them. Don't resist these moments. Let them be. It sometimes

105

might not be possible to change part of your routine or schedule, however, what's important is that you balance your routine and make time for yourself, for relaxation and for self-reflection. You can do this by taking nature walks in the local park. You can also do this by taking a warm bath at the end of the day, or maybe a massage during the middle of the day can help extinguish stress, anxiety and worry from your body.

Consider also taking time to nourish your spirit throughout the day with prayer, meditation, Yoga, Tai Chi and other practices that will help you keep your emotions calm, relaxed and centered. It doesn't really matter what you do, as long as for short periods of time throughout your day you can find the time to unwind a little to help you gain some perspective about your life and circumstances.

Use the Power of Visualization - Visualization is a fantastic method for grounding yourself during times of intense emotional turmoil and uncertainty.

Find a quiet place without distractions where you can lie down or at the very least sit down comfortably. If that's not possible, then sit where you are or lie down on the floor while listening to tranquil music. Initially, allow your mind to wander and just find its place in the moment. However, after a few minutes take control of the images forming in your imagination and imagine a tranquil place - a sanctuary of sorts that you can escape to. This is a place filled with all the things that make you feel comfortable, at peace and relaxed.

Spend five to ten minutes at a time exploring this place, relaxing within this imaginary world, and allowing all your stresses and worries to melt away. In fact, use the time you have within this sanctuary to think about your life, circumstances, and problems. Just maybe within this place, you will find the necessary perspective and the answers you need to help you get through the pressures of life. Later, whenever you feel stressed or overwhelmed, take some time to come back to this place to help ground yourself during moments of uncertainty.

Learn About Breath Control - While visualizing and/or meditating, it's important that you breathe correctly in ways that will help you to relax and center yourself emotionally. Deep diaphragmatic breathing is one method used that can help you maintain your composure and relax your body.

Diaphragmatic breathing requires that you breathe in through your diaphragm for four seconds, then hold your breath for another four seconds, and then breathe out for the final four seconds, and then begin again. Doing this for up to five minutes at a time can help you feel more centered and relaxed. With more emotional composure, you will find the strength you need to move through your problems successfully.

Use the Power of Metaphors - Metaphors are absolutely wonderful tools you can use to help gain a proper perspective on the problems and circumstances confronting your reality. Use them to help you see your problems in a different light. Or use them to find more strength and comfort in the moment.

Metaphors will provide you with a different view of yourself and your circumstances. This shift of perspective might be all you need to stay relaxed, calm and composed during pressure situations.

For instance, your natural tendency and instinct might be to panic a little when you're suddenly confronted with an unexpected problem. In such instances, you will most likely blow the problem out of proportion, which will have a tendency to overwhelm your senses, while also causing you emotional distress. Instead of picturing your problem as this gigantic mountain that you now must climb, imagine it instead as a tiny ant. See it as a tiny little ant walking beneath your feet.

The benefit of looking at your problem in this way is that you are no longer seeing it as this big dragon that you must slay. Instead, you are imagining it as something small - as something you can easily control and influence. This will have a tendency to calm your mind while helping you gain the proper perspective you need to solve this problem.

Another metaphor you could use is to imagine your problem as mouldable clay. Here your problem is no longer this stiff titanium wall that's standing between you and your desired outcome. Instead, it's something you can mold and reshape to your heart's content.

In the previous couple of examples you were using metaphors for your problems, however, imagine you could now also use metaphors. For instance, imagine yourself as water. Or imagine yourself as a soaring bird. Or imagine yourself as gentle clouds rolling across the sky. Ask yourself:

• How would I approach this problem if I was liquid water?

• What new perspectives could I gain if I was a soaring eagle?

• What if I approached this problem from the perspective of a gentle rolling cloud?

These metaphors will certainly not always provide you with instant answers. They do require some thought and contemplation. Answers and new perspectives will come the more life you give to each of the metaphors you use. What's most important is that you use them to help separate yourself from the problem in order to gain some new and unique insights and perspectives that will help you to move forward in a more positive way.

Build Your Emotional Coping Skills - Building your emotional coping skills means you are learning to manage to proactively handle your emotional responses. This often begins with developing a deeper understanding of the meaning of each of your emotions, and of your emotional tendencies.

Succeeding here means that you will no longer be at the mercy of your emotions. You will instead be in control of your emotional destiny. No longer will pressure situations or problems overwhelm you because you have finally become a fully aware and present individual who understands and appreciates the value that every emotion has to offer.

Building your emotional coping skills will, of course, take some time and effort. However, everything worthwhile takes time. It is after all only within each experience that you will find the lessons you need to help build your emotional intelligence.

Long-term Lifestyle Changes to Help You Stay Calm

In order to become a more serene, calm and peaceful person in the long-run, it's important that you make some long-term lifestyle changes that will provide you with the ability to more readily control your emotional responses. However, it's not only about the lifestyle, it's also about the mindset you bring into every moment of your life. In fact, both lifestyle and mindset

110

go hand-in-hand and work together to help you stay calm under pressure.

Here are some suggestions to help you stay calm under pressure for the long-term:

Get Good Quality Sleep and Exercise - Good quality sleep and exercise is absolutely paramount. Getting good quality sleep will help you become much more emotionally resilient. Likewise, regular exercise will provide you with the energy you need to consciously and physically work through difficulties far more effectively.

When you're well rested and when your body is feeling fit, you will naturally have a more calming energy about you. It will be much easier for you to stay relaxed during uncertain times and difficult moments. You will find yourself feeling more centered, focused and in control. This will provide you with the clarity of mind you need to work through emotional issues far more successfully.

Eat a Well Balanced Diet - Moving on from the previous point, it's also very important to eat well. Eating a well balanced and healthy diet, keeping yourself hydrated with water throughout the day, and avoiding the habit of indulging in addictions will help you to manage your emotions, and your responses to the events and circumstances of your life far more effectively.

In particular avoid drugs, alcohol, sugar and caffeine addictions. These addictions will put you on edge, making it very difficult to stay calm and centered throughout the day.

Spend Time Simplifying Your Life - It's difficult to stay calm and centered when you're living in a complicated mess. When there's too much clutter, when you're constantly trying to find things, when you have too many commitments and responsibilities — far more then you can handle — that is when things become very messy. This is a clear indication that your life is far too complicated. It's very difficult to find calmness from within if you live in a hectic and complex world.

Commit yourself today to the process of simplifying your life and environment. For instance, take time to organize yourself and your things. Make sure to find a place for everything, and put everything in its place. Be sure to de-clutter your environment, to eliminate all non-essential things, or simply pack them away out of sight and out of mind.

It's also important to avoid living a frantic lifestyle. Having too many commitments and responsibilities don't give you enough time for yourself and your own emotional needs. What you need is space, and a clean uncluttered environment to help you unwind, relax, and calm down. This is the sort of environment that will encourage moments of self-reflection that you can use to help improve your decisions moving forward.

Physically Slow Down - Living at a frantic pace can work quite well for some people. In fact, there are people who thrive on urgency, while still maintaining a calm and centered energy. However, this kind of lifestyle isn't for everyone because it can lead to high levels of stress and anxiety.

If you typically suffer from stress and anxiety throughout your day, then it's a clear indication that you are living too frantically. There's just too much going on in your life, and at the moment you're just unable to handle yourself or your circumstances. In such instances, it's important to begin slowing things down. This, of course, isn't easy. There's just so much to do and so little time. However, what you must do is re-prioritize things in order to help create the space and time you need to slow down.

Slowing down doesn't necessarily mean that you do everything more slowly. It does, however, mean that you do things more consciously. Therefore instead of rushing through a task, think through the task and take a little time to consider how to best work on this task in the most effective and time-efficient way.

Slowing down also means finding time for periods of relaxation. It means taking regular thought-breaks. Thought-breaks are times throughout the day when you take several minutes to separate yourself from your tasks and activities to just sit down and think about your decisions and actions. These moments of self-reflection could very well provide you with some interesting insights that will help you work much more productively moving forward.

Consistently Build Your Support Network - During moments of great emotional upheaval, it's important to have people whom you can talk to and reach out to. These people are part of your support network. They are there to assist you during difficult moments of your life, and you are also there to assist them in their emotional and physical struggles.

Take some time now to consider the kind of people that could add value to your life. Also, consider the people you could readily assist and support. Jot down the names of all these individuals and commit yourself to regularly staying in touch with them. You could even create an emotional Mastermind group. This is where you invite like-minded individuals to a get-together once a week or month where you discuss problems, concerns, and other emotional struggles.

Your support network will provide you with an anchor you can use during difficult emotional moments of your life. They will instill within you the calmness you need when there are emotional storms brewing around you.

Prepare for Difficulties in Advance - One of the best ways to stay calm, focused and centered at all times, is to prepare for seemingly unexpected setbacks, difficulties, and problems in advance. Of course, you might be thinking that if something is unexpected, then there's absolutely no way to prepare for it. Therefore let's look at it another way: Taking time to think about and preparing for possible future scenarios brings them from the realm of the "unknown" into your conscious awareness. Therefore, what was unexpected before, is now something you are ready to tackle in the moment or in the future.

When you have a full and complete awareness of what you are going to do in the next moment when things change, you will naturally be more calm, collected and emotionally centered. It's often those unexpected moments when events and circumstances catch you by surprise that lead to emotional upheaval and overwhelm. However, given the fact that you are now prepared for the possibilities, you will, therefore, be in a much more favorable position to stay calm and collected during these difficult moments of your life.

Think Through Your Decisions in Advance - Moving on from the previous point, it's also important that you reflect upon the consequences of your choices, decisions, and actions in advance. It's very possible that certain decisions can lead you down one path, and other decisions will lead you down a completely different path. Both of these paths have consequences and certain outcomes that you must keep in mind. Some of these outcomes might lead you into an emotional tornado, while other outcomes might be a little more favorable.

115

Taking into consideration the short and long-term possibilities of your choices and decisions will put you in the driver's seat of your life. Your mind will be prepared and ready to deal with numerous scenarios and situations. And when your mind is prepared, your emotions will be steady and you will respond proactively to the events and circumstances of your life. This will leave you feeling calmer and centered moving forward.

One of the best ways to identify the potential consequences of your choices and decisions is to simply take some time to sit and reflect in a quiet place. Just sit, and visualize "if I make this choice right now, it will most likely result in…" Take time to consider all the possibilities, and then prepare yourself mentally and physically for all the possible outcomes.

⁇

CHAPTER 11: BREATHING THERAPY

Breathing exercises are an excellent, quick and easy solution for stress and anxiety relief. Proper breathing techniques work on anxiety on a physiological level by automatically slowing your heart rate. The effect on anger is almost instant. Because calm breathing is a physiological strategy, this approach is also virtually universally effective for getting anger relief. It's hard to go wrong with it.

Don't wait until fight-or-flight kicks in before minding the breath. Controlled breathing not only keeps your mind and body functioning at their best, it can also lower blood pressure, promote feelings of calm and relaxation, and help you de-stress. While the effects of breathing therapy on anger haven't been studied at length at least in a controlled clinical setting, many experts encourage using the breath as a means of increasing awareness, mindfulness, or for to find that elusive state of Zen.

Breathing exercises can make you dizzy or lightheaded, so be careful and use caution. If a specific exercise recommends sitting to perform it, it is important that you comply. There are lots of breathing exercises you can do to help relax. The first exercise below - equal breathing - is simple to learn and easy to do. It's best to start there if you have never done breathing exercises before. The other exercises are more advanced. All of these exercises can help you relax and relieve stress. From the confines of a bed, a desk, or anywhere negativity finds its way, consider these six techniques to help keep calm and carry on.

Equal Breathing

How it's done: Balance can do a body good, beginning with the breath. To start, inhale for a count of four, then exhale for a count of four (all through the nose, which adds a natural resistance to the breath). Got the basic pranayama down? More advanced yogis can aim for six to eight counts per breath with the same goal in mind: Calm the nervous system, increase focus, and reduce stress.

When it works best: Anytime, anyplace - but this is one technique that's especially effective before bed. Similar to counting sheep, if you're having trouble falling asleep, this breath can help take your mind off the racing thoughts, or whatever might be distracting you.

Abdominal Breathing Technique

How it's done: With one hand on the chest and the other on the belly, take a deep breath in through the nose, ensuring the diaphragm (not the chest) inflates with enough air to create a stretch in the lungs. The goal: Six to 10 deep, slow breaths per minute for 10 minutes each day to experience immediate reductions to heart rate and blood pressure. Keep at it for six to eight weeks, and those benefits might stick around even longer.

When it works best: Before an exam or any stressful event. But keep in mind, those who operate in a stressed state all the time might be a little shocked how hard it is to control the breath. To help train the breath, consider biofeedback tools which can help you pace your breathing.

Peaceful Breathing

Stand or sit. Relax your body and try to calm your mind. Inhale slowly through your nose while counting slowly to four. Exhale slowly through your mouth while counting to six. Hold the breath for a couple of seconds, and then let the air out steadily. You should try to exhale completely. Don't hunch your shoulders, and as you breathe in, let the air expand down into your abdomen. Repeat several times.

Belly Breathing

Lay on the floor. You can use a pillow to prevent your lower back from straining. The function of breathing occurs when the diaphragm – the muscle that separates your lungs from your abdominal cavity – is drawn down, and your lungs can expand. By lying on your back, you can use your hands to find the bottom of your rib cage and, as you inhale, apply light pressure on your abdomen toward the bottom of your body. Allow yourself to feel your belly expand as you draw in your breath; that's the way you draw in the fullest possible breath and expand the lungs. Belly breathing is much healthier breathing than chest breathing, where only the upper portion of the lungs is being used at full capacity. Repeat this breathing exercise for 10 to 15 minutes.

Reverse Breathe

Sit with your back firmly upright and your shoulders squared. Exhale – before you take a breath – completely. Push as much air out of your lungs as you can. Draw in a full breath – a real belly breath. Once you feel as though you've drawn in all the air you can, force yourself to draw in slightly more air. You should feel the expansion in your belly and through your rib cage. Hold for one or two seconds, then release slowly. Pull in your abdominal muscles as tight as you can, while you are exhaling. Repeat five to 10 times.

Humming

Repeat the steps for the reverse breath above; however, this time, as you exhale, hum lightly as you exhale. Be sure to squeeze your abdominal muscles as tightly as possible while exhaling and humming.

Short Breaths

This is one of the exercises that may be more likely to cause light-headedness, so be sure to stay seated while doing this exercise. To begin, sit on a chair with your spine straight and your shoulders squared. Without exhaling in between, draw in three short breaths through your nose. Hold for two to three seconds, then release and exhale through the mouth. Immediately repeat. Repeat the entire exercise four to six times. Stop if you become light-headed.

Puffing

Puffing exhales puts a bit of pressure on your lungs, making the airway stay open a bit longer. It's a great method to use if you are exercising heavily and feeling out of breath. To do this exercise, either sit or stand with your back straight. Inhale deeply, filling your lungs. As you exhale, puff your cheeks and blow the air out of your mouth through tightened, pursed lips. It should take you three to four times as long to exhale the air as it did to inhale the air. Repeat four to six times.

Waking Breath

This is a great breathing exercise to do if you are feeling drowsy at work and think you might doze off. It also exercises your diaphragm, a key muscle in the function of breathing. In this exercise, you should remain seated. You will be breathing in and out through the nose, keeping the mouth shut but not tensed. Only do the exercise for about 10 seconds at a time, since it may make you light-headed. To perform the exercise, inhale short breaths through your nose and immediately exhale them through your nose. Repeat for 10 seconds, then stop and breathe normally. Do for 10 seconds out of every minute for 10 minutes.

Breath Bends

This exercise will help you empty your lungs completely so that you can improve the amount of oxygen you intake. Stand with your feet shoulder-width apart, with your back straight and your knees relaxed. Inhale deeply. As you exhale, bend at the waist, forcing as much air out of your lungs as possible. Straighten back up as you inhale and continue to repeat four to six times, or until you get too light-headed to continue.

Progressive Relaxation

How it's done: To nix tension from head to toe, close the eyes and focus on tensing and relaxing each muscle group for two to three seconds each. Start with the feet and toes, then move up to the knees, thighs, glutes, chest, arms, hands, neck, jaw, and eyes - all while maintaining deep, slow breaths. Having trouble staying on track? Breathe in through the nose, hold for a count of five while the muscles tense, then breathe out through the mouth on release.

When it works best: At home, at a desk, or even on the road. One word of caution: Dizziness is never the goal. If holding the breath ever feels uncomfortable, tone it down to just a few seconds.

Alternate Nostril Breathing

How it's done: A yogi's best friend, this breath is said to bring calm, balance, and unite the right and left sides of the brain. Starting in a comfortable meditative pose, hold the right thumb over the right nostril and inhale deeply through the left nostril. At the peak of inhalation, close off the left nostril with the ring finger, then exhale through the right nostril. Continue the pattern, inhaling through the right nostril, closing it off with the right thumb, and exhaling through the left nostril.

When it works best: Crunch time, or whenever it's time to focus or energize. Just don't try this one before bed: It "clears the channels" and make people feel more awake. It's almost like a cup of coffee.

Guided Visualization

How it's done: Head straight for your happy place, no questions asked. With a coach, therapist, or helpful recording as your guide, breathe deeply while focusing on pleasant, positive images to replace any negative thoughts. While it's just one means of achieving mindfulness, guided visualization helps puts you in the place you want to be, rather than letting your mind go to the internal dialogue that is stressful.

When it works best: pretty much any place you can safely close your eyes and let go.

Skull Shining Breath

How it's done: Ready to brighten up your day from the inside out? This one begins with a long, slow inhale, followed by a quick, powerful exhale generated from the lower belly. Once comfortable with the contraction, up the pace to one inhale-exhale (all through the nose) every one to two seconds, for a total of 10 breaths.

When it works best: When it's time to wake up or start looking on the bright side. It's pretty abdominal-intensive, but it will warm up the body, shake off stale energy, and wake up the brain. If alternate nostril breathing is like coffee, consider this a shot of espresso.

⏃

CHAPTER 12: PERSONALITY DISORDER - HOW TO RECOGNIZE IT

The word 'personality' refers to the pattern of thoughts, feelings, and behavior that makes each of us the individuals that we are. These affect the way we think, feel and behave towards ourselves and others.

We don't always think, feel and behave in exactly the same way – it depends on the situation we are in, the people with us and many other things. But we mostly tend to behave in fairly predictable ways. Personality disorders are a type of mental health problem where your attitudes, beliefs, and behaviors cause longstanding problems in your life. Your experience of personality disorder is unique to you. However, you may often experience difficulties in how you think about yourself and others. You may find it difficult to change these unwanted patterns.

What Causes Personality Disorders?

Personality disorders develop in childhood and the thoughts and behaviors become increasingly ingrained in adulthood.

Some personality disorders are more common in men (i.e. antisocial personality disorder) and others are more common in women (i.e. borderline personality disorder).

Many people with a personality disorder do not seek help until after years of distress, if at all. This contributes to our lack of knowledge about their causes and development. Different causes appear to be associated with the different types of personality disorders. However, like most mental illnesses, the causes appear to be a complex combination of genetic factors, biochemical factors, and individual, family, and environmental factors.

What Are The Signs Of A Personality Disorder?

You might be given a diagnosis of personality disorder if all three of these apply:

•   The way you think, feel and behave causes you or other significant problems in daily life. For example, you may feel unable to trust others or you may often feel abandoned, causing you or others unhappiness.

•   The way you think, feel and behave causes significant problems across different aspects of your life. You may struggle to start or keep friendships, to control your feelings and behavior or get on with people at work, for example.

•   These problems continue for a long time. These difficult patterns may have started when you were a child or teenager and can carry on into your life as an adult.

You may welcome your diagnosis, finding it a way to make sense of your experience. Or you may find it more difficult to come to terms with.

The Main Types Of Personality Disorder

There is a wide range of personality disorders. All of them involve a pervasive pattern of behavior, which means that the characteristic behaviors and thoughts are evident in almost all aspects of a person's life. There are three clusters of personality disorders: odd or eccentric disorders; dramatic, emotional or erratic disorders; and anxious or fearful disorders. Specific disorders are as follows:

Paranoid personality disorder is a pervasive distrust and suspiciousness of others, such that their motives are interpreted as malevolent.

Schizoid personality disorder is a pervasive pattern of detachment from social relationships and a restricted range of expression of emotions in interpersonal settings.

126

Schizotypal personality disorder is a pervasive pattern of social and interpersonal deficits marked by acute discomfort with reduced capacity for close relationships. It is also characterized by distortions of thinking and perception and eccentric behavior.

Antisocial personality disorder is a pervasive pattern of disregard for and violation of the rights of others.

Histrionic personality disorder is a pervasive pattern of excessive emotion and attention seeking.

Narcissistic personality disorder is a pervasive pattern of grandiosity (in fantasy or actual behavior), need for admiration, and lack of empathy.

Avoidant personality disorder is a pervasive pattern of social inhibition, feelings of inadequacy, and hypersensitivity to negative evaluation.

Dependent personality disorder is a pervasive and excessive need to be taken care of, which leads to submissive and clinging behavior and fears of separation.

Obsessive-compulsive personality disorder is a pervasive pattern of preoccupation with orderliness, perfectionism, and mental and interpersonal control, at the expense of flexibility, openness, and efficiency.

Borderline personality disorder is a pervasive pattern of instability of interpersonal relationships, self-image, moods, and control over impulses.

127

Understanding borderline personality disorder is particularly important because it can be misdiagnosed as another mental illness, particularly a mood disorder.

People with borderline personality disorder are likely to have:

• Wide mood swings.

• Inappropriate anger or difficulty controlling anger.

• Chronic feelings of emptiness.

• Recurrent suicidal behavior, gestures or threats, or self-harming behavior.

• Impulsive and self-destructive behavior.

• A pattern of unstable relationships.

• Persistent unstable self-image or sense of self.

• Fear of abandonment.

• Periods of paranoia and loss of contact with reality.

⏎

CHAPTER 13: MEDITATIONS TECHNIQUES

The crucial skill of meditation is learning to focus, to be completely concentered. As your whole being gets engrossed in meditation, every tension and stress of daily life will fall from your shoulders. In barely a couple of seconds, you will feel rested and refreshed. Your mental attitude will be more constructive and compassionate. Your family and colleagues will immediately see the benefits of your meditation. You'll attain best conclusions, have greater creativity, and become playfully adroit in dealing the challenges of the day. The world is full of exhausted, ill-natured, stressed-out persons trying to be the best, attempting to do the correct thing, trying to equilibrize their career and bring up a healthy family. Meditation helps you make an honest, loving attitude so that you can endure even the hardest or most intense times.

On a regular basis meditating will help you feel positive about your day-to-day life, rejuvenated, and spiritually attuned. Meditation is a great source for preventing feelings of distress and overwhelm, frustrations that often stem from modern-day stresses. We scurry from place to place, troubled by our cellular phone and our pagers, consumed by the demand and convenience of e-mail. We have so much to pay attention to that the priority of our relationship with ourselves, the most significant relationship of all, is badly ignored. The fact that you're curious about meditation Signifies that it's not too late to begin your journey towards a healthier, better lifestyle. You must remember that you're the foundation of all that swirls around you. When you are spiritually Fit, you will be able to serve other people. Have in mind the saying by President Lincoln, "You don't strengthen the weak by weakening the strong." Every building bears a base. The larger the building, the Firmer the base. Once the building is fully built, the foundation is covered. It is buried deep into the earth, even though it holds the entire construction. Try to look at building your own spiritual strength in this manner. When we forget our roots, our foundation, life is full of stress and fear. Only by diving deep inside can we reconnect with our own roots, our own foundation.

Meditation is a scientific discipline of self-discovery, self-understanding, and self-transformation. By meditation, we recollect who we're and hence, regain our dignity and our love for life. This is among the significant reasons why meditation is a basic, foundational issue for all of us. We have to devote attention.

How to Get Started With Meditation in 5 Easy Steps

Step 1: Prepare Your Space.

First things first: select your spot. Find somewhere quiet and peaceful, where you won't be disturbed during your meditation. This might be your bedroom, home office, or anywhere that you can close the door and find uninterrupted solitude. As you practice meditation, it will become easier to practice anywhere, but as you are first getting started, quiet and solitude are very beneficial. Once you've settled on a location, make sure that your meditation spot is neat and clean. A messy, cluttered space can make it harder to relax and focus. While not required, you might also find it helpful to set the mood by lighting a candle or stick of incense, or playing some soft, ambient music - whatever helps you get "in the zone."

Step 2. Set a Goal.

Starting a meditation practice can be challenging to people, especially in our fast-paced world. I find that it is extremely helpful to decide in advance how long you are going to practice so that you have accountability from the beginning. I recommend 20-40 minutes per session, depending on how comfortable you are in your practice; adjust as needed. It's important to note that distractions are inevitable, and that is okay. Do what you can to minimize them (turn off your phone, let your roommates/family know what you're up to, etc.). If you are interrupted for whatever reason, just sit back down and finish your session as soon as you can. The biggest hurdle by far, especially in the beginning, is not distractions, but your own mind and restlessness. The ego can't stand sitting quietly, doing nothing, and it will come up with an endless list of things you should or could be doing instead. Don't give in. Set a timer, or a stopwatch, or an alarm on your phone, and don't dismiss your meditation until your settled-upon time has been reached.

Step 3. Get Comfortable.

When I say "get comfortable", I am speaking in the literal sense. Posture is important in meditation, for many reasons. It helps you breathe easier and deeper. It helps the flow and circulation of blood and energy. Perhaps most importantly, sitting properly will help to minimize aches, pains, and discomfort. There is not one correct way to sit; this depends on your body type, bone structure, and constitution. You can sit on the floor, on a cushion or a bench. You can sit in a chair, or even stand up if that's easier. The important thing is not to slouch or lean against anything. You should be relaxed yet poised, loose yet balanced, comfortable but alert. Pay attention to any pain or discomfort in your back or your legs, and make adjustments as necessary. It takes time, but eventually, you will find the "sweet spot," where your spine is erect, but not rigid; straight, but not stiff. The perfect balance of effort and ease.

Step 4. Follow the Breath.

Bring your attention to your breathing. Focus on the sensations: the air flowing in and out of your mouth and nostrils; the rise and fall of your chest, the filling, and emptying of your belly. Don't try to control your breathing. No need to deliberately breathe slow or deep (although this will often happen on its own, as you become aware of your breathing). Just pay attention, and feel the rhythm, the ebb, and flow. There are breathing exercises which we will explore later on, but for now, just observe.

Step 5. Just Relax.

Easier said than done, right? But relaxing is possible, and the first step is awareness. Start by becoming aware of any places in your body where there is tension or discomfort. We have a tendency to store stress in our bodies, particularly in the legs, shoulders, back, neck, and face. Each time you breathe out, imagine that tension flowing out of your body. With every breath, release and relax, until you feel entirely comfortable and at ease. This can take some time, especially as you are first getting started. Generally, the more often you practice, the quicker and easier it will be to let go of stress and sink into a state of peace and relaxation.

Meditation Techniques You Can Use

There are several different meditation techniques that a person can practice. The important thing is to find a meditation technique that you are comfortable with and try to stick with that one. If you tend to bounce around from one meditation technique to the other you will not get the full benefits of meditation. Meditation has many benefits both physically, psychologically and spiritually. Some of these include control anger, lower blood pressure, improved skin tone, happy outlook on life, less stress and just an overall feeling of wellbeing. Today we are just going to give a brief outline of five of the major meditation techniques.

Trataka

The first meditation technique we want to talk about is Trataka Meditation. Trataka in Sanskrit means to look or gaze. When performing Trataka Meditation a person fixes their gaze on an external object. This can be a dot on the wall, candle flame or whatever. Trataka Meditation is an ancient yoga practiced to develop concentration and the Ajna (third eye) chakra. Basically, the person gazes at the object till the eyes begin to water. As they are gazing they let all thoughts flow through their mind and pass away. Once the eyes begin to water the eyes are then closed. When Trataka Meditation is performed with a candle after the eyes begin to water and are closed the person concentrates on the image of the flame. At first, this will be an after image but will fade into seeing the image with the mind's eye. This is a good way to develop the third eye chakra.

Mantra

The next meditation technique is Mantra Meditation. Mantra Meditation is where you say a word such as ohm over and over in your mind. In Mantra Meditation the word acts like a vehicle that takes you to a state of no thought. When repeating the mantra or word it is very common for the mind to drift off into other thoughts. When this happens the person needs to gentle bring their thoughts back to the mantra and start repeating it once again. In Mantra Meditation the word that is repeated is specific for the purpose of transforming the person in a spiritual way. Typically a mantra will be given to a mediator by a guru.

Chakra

The third meditation technique is Chakra Meditation. There are seven major chakras in the human body. When performing Chakra Meditation the person will focus on a specific chakra for the purpose of cleansing or energizing that chakra. Chakra Meditation has the ability to revitalize a person's body through the cleansing, revitalizing process. As the chakras are interrelated it is advised to start with the root chakra and work your way up when performing Chakra Meditation. When doing Chakra Meditation you can also use the aid of crystals to help in the cleansing, revitalization process. Chakra Meditation can be a powerful meditation for healing and the clearing of negative emotions.

Vipassana

The forth meditation technique is Vipassana Meditation. Vipassana Meditation is one of the oldest forms of meditation and is used for the purpose of gaining insight into one's nature and the nature of reality. The goal of Vipassana Meditation is to bring suffering to an end for the individual. This is accomplished by eliminating the three conditions which are impermanence, suffering, and not-self. After practicing Vipassana Meditation for a long period the meditator is supposed to come to a point where they separate these three conditions from themselves and achieving nirvana. It is believed that all physical and psychological conditions are not part of the true self or the "I" and should be eliminated with the practice of Vipassana Meditation.

Raja

The last meditation technique we will talk about is Raja Meditation. In Raja Meditation the mind is considered king and it is the minds job to tame the emotions and the body. Raja Meditation attempts to have the mind bring the body and emotions under complete control. Raja Meditation and the associated practices is a very disciplined type of meditation. When a person takes up Raja Meditation they are expected to give up things like anger, sex, alcohol, meat and pay close attention to their actions. The idea in Raja Meditation for giving up these things is it prepares the body and mind for meditation.

I hope you will put your all into those meditations. After all, you deserve peace and happiness. And the meditations above are very beneficial

To get the most out of those meditations, use these tips.

• Understand that anger is a feeling created by yourself. Sure, certain external events can lead us to anger, but the ultimate feeling, anger itself, is created by ourselves. An important part of Buddhist meditation is to recognize that we, ourselves, create our emotions. In fact, the best way to gain control of your feelings and emotions is to understand that you yourself are creating them. Take a look at my guide to controlling your feelings and emotions for more on this.

• Understand that anger is a product of the mind. That's why the only way to stop being angry is to control the mind. And that's really what meditation is, its total self-control. It's self-mastery. Naturally, self-mastery is not so easy. It's a challenge. Buddha meditated for decades before attaining enlightenment under the Bodhi tree. But we don't need to achieve enlightenment to manage our anger. We just need a bit of control.

• Accept reality as it is. To do this, simply focus your mind 100% on any part of your present environment. For instance, if you're walking home from work and you're angry, just focus your mind 100% on what you're doing: walking. Your anger will chill like cinders on the snow.

⬚

CHAPTER 14: ANGER MANAGEMENT THE LAW OF ATTRACTION WAY

The Law of Attraction states that you create what you think about the most. So in other words if you think about, and dwell on, negative thoughts you will manifest situations and people, in your life, that will promote bad feeling or unpleasant experiences. All outcomes however, are controlled by you, so you always possess the power to change the negative aspects in your life for more positive ones. All you need to do is learn a few attracting techniques.

One of the misconceptions about law of attraction is you must get all manically happy immediately or you are royally fucked when it comes to manifesting what you want. Sure, you want everything you want because you believe getting it will make you feel good, and since we can only attract into our experience that which we are a match to now energetically, we have to work on feeling good in the present moment, and not insist on maintaining our misery until what we want gets here. That was a mouthful wasn't it?

So, yes, you have to allow yourself to start feeling better no matter what your current reality looks like , no matter 'what is' in this present moment. But, that doesn't mean just suppressing all the negativity and pretending it isn't there. It isn't about going into denial, and trying to convince yourself you believe all these wonderful beliefs that you really don't. You have to actually genuinely feel better, and that can be a process. If you have been in a depressive funk for the last six months where you have seriously considered jumping off a bridge, you won't be able to just jump right to a vibration of 'life is so great, the sun is shining and I'm just so happy to be alive.'

Energy responds to energy and positive vibrations will therefore be responsive to positive feelings, whilst negative vibrations will stick to feelings of doom and gloom. Every single mood or feeling that you experience will create a positive or negative vibration, and this is what the Law of Attraction responds to – the way you are feeling at any given moment. This is why when you are in a bad mood more unpleasant things or situations seem to occur or appear to head your way.

Understanding that it is the mood you choose to feel, at any moment, that influences how you will be feeling will enable you to have more control over the amount of negative/positive experiences you have. Thinking positive thoughts, and creating a good feeling inside will draw you towards other experiences that will continue to encourage you to keep feeling this way.

To get more of the positive things that you want in your life, and less of the negative stuff that you're not quite so keen on, you need to understand how to use the Law of Attraction. If you are feeling angry or aggressive your vibration will be negative. If you continue to feel this way you will begin to attract people, situations and experiences that are on the same vibrational level as you. This means that the happy, positive feelings you would like to be enjoying are being blocked by negative vibrations, and will continue to be repelled until you actively change your vibration by choosing to alter your mood or feeling.

A lot of people who have started working more consciously with their energy report difficulty in really making shifts in their energy. The negative emotion has such a strong pull, and it is so hard to feel better in the midst of all the unwanted things in their current experience. A lot of crap has built up over the years and letting it rise to the surface to be dealt with can be unpleasant. Most of us aren't very comfortable expressing our negative emotion. We are taught it isn't appropriate to express it in many cases.

And this is especially true of anger. It is a nasty, ugly emotion that should be bottled up. We really weren't taught it was okay to feel angry, and as such, we never learned how to express it constructively. Many anger releases are very destructive, and since that is what we tend to see most of the time, this only adds to the idea that anger is bad. Suppressed anger is a major cause of so much turmoil in this world.

Many people on a spiritual path may feel that they should be past anger and it isn't an emotion that people operating on a higher level of consciousness should be experiencing. While I am sure there are some people that have managed to achieve this feat, overall I think this is kind of bullshit. We can certainly make strides in this area without a doubt, and experience it less often and less intensely, but the idea we should strive to eliminate an emotion completely seems a bit much to me. All emotions have value in that they show us where we are focusing our energy. Yes, anger is intense and unpleasant and if we can work through our emotional turmoil without getting to that point, awesome. But that always doesn't happen and we are angry, plain and simple.

It is not something to be suppressed. It is something that we have every right to feel and express, we just want to do it in a constructive way. There is great value in anger and it can be an incredibly healing emotion...like incredibly, you have no idea.

You are supremely pissed my friend. It is easy to miss the connection though. Feelings of depression and numbness are quite muted, and your energy may feel kind of thick and heavy. Anger has so much charge to it and feels intense. The energy feels more 'buzzy' and quick-moving. But that is without a doubt what is happening. There has been so much shit you have been ignoring or stuffing down, deeper and deeper, the anger has retreated to the deeper recesses of your

141

being. But it is still there, alive and well. There is a part of you that is aware of it, but to dive in feels absolutely terrifying. The extreme lack of energy that comes with these types of emotional states is also a contributing factor to the continued ignoring and suppressing...you literally don't have the energy to deal with your feelings. If you want to move past these states, the anger release will help you do that like nothing else. You have no idea. But, in order to reap the benefits, you have to be willing to examine what is happening inside. What are you angry about?

Once you figure that out and let yourself feel it, you will start feeling a lot better. You probably won't feel great. You'll open up a few more 'can of worms' emotionally speaking, but you'll open up some energy, and that sense of hopelessness that comes from feeling depressed and numb, will begin to lift.

In our efforts to better ourselves and be happier and more peaceful, we pick up all sorts of awesome nuggets of truth and wisdom that can completely transform our lives, like learning to cultivate compassion for the people who have hurt us because their acts were borne of their own pain and unhappiness, taking responsibility for our life, and completely owing our feelings and never blaming others for making us feel a certain way. But, when it comes to really healing ourselves, and releasing the energies that are interfering with the transformations

142

we want to make, and disallowing what we want to show up in our lives, this shit just isn't going to help.

Trying to reach for these perspectives when you are nowhere near them,is just going to shut down a lot of 'stuff' that needs to come up, along with the insights and clarity that always accompanies these 'moments of truth.' Anger releases are not the time to try and be all enlightened. This is the time to let out all the shit that you are angry about. It doesn't matter how petty, irrational, mean or hurtful a thought seems. It doesn't matter how much you should 'know better' than to be angry about some of the things you are angry about. This is the time to just let yourself be supremely pissed about all the things about which you are pissed, plain and simple.

Be mad at your mom for being a shitty parent and making your childhood miserable. Be mad at your ex-boyfriend for leaving you. Be mad that you think your race, religion or sexual orientation has made your life more difficult and has held you back in some way.

Be mad that you're broke and miserable, and can't do any of the things you want to do. Be mad that you know how awesome your products or services are, and that nobody seems to be buying them. Be mad that people who are not as smart or talented as you are so much more successful.

Be mad that your special needs child wasn't born 'normal' and it totally turned your life upside down. Be mad at your husband for taking terrible care of himself and checking out on you much earlier than expected.

So this means you don't necessarily have to confront people that have made you angry in some way. The point of anger release is to cleanse your energy field a bit and facilitate healing. How we respond to everything in our life is all about us anyway, and when we really let that truth sink in, we realize the confrontations, the apologies, explanations of why people did what they did, and so on, are not a necessary part of the process.

Now this isn't to say there can't be any benefit to talking with others and letting them know how you feel. It may very well have a variety of positive outcomes, such as healing a relationship that has been fractured or getting a sense of closure from finally saying your piece. But if you are feeling pretty fragile and raw right now, this may not be the best time to do this. But if you were to go this route, you have to realize you can't make your feeling better dependent on this person responding in a certain way. The apologies, the acknowledgments of your feelings and what have you can certainly make you feel better, and it is understandable to want them, but they may not come. If you do feel the urge to confront, discuss and what not, I would highly recommend doing some work on yourself first and getting into a better space mentally and emotionally. Let some of the pain heal. Let some of the resentment fade away.

Sibling rivalry, political disappointments, workplace issues, abuse, betrayal, and infidelity are just a few of the many reasons that people have for harboring feelings of anger and resentment. Although anger is an emotion that is as natural as any other, it has a tendency to eat away at the soul of the person who does not understand its role in their lives.

Yes, anger does have its place and everyone will experience it. In fact, this emotion is highly beneficial to us at times. However, you do yourself a grave disservice by remaining angry. Holding onto anger until it becomes bitter resentment is a fail-safe way to disallow the benefits of Universal Law of Attraction. Ask yourself if that is what you want. You may be justified in your disapproval of the circumstances or events that led to your anger. Maybe someone was unfair, inconsiderate, or downright evil to you. You may have been 100% right and they may have been 100% wrong; but the person causing the most harm to you now is none other than you.

Your anger is not harming the person to whom it is directed. In fact, many people spend decades being angry with someone who barely remembers the event that caused the anger. That person's life will not be changed by your anger, but yours will.

By not overcoming what you think and feel about the circumstances surrounding your anger, you give up your own power. You hold yourself in a state of mind that is not in alignment with your life purpose. You make it almost impossible to enjoy the manifestations of your desires because of the resistant thoughts that fill your mind. The key question: Are they worth it? Are the people who have wronged you worth the price that you are paying? Keep reading if the answer is no.

The first step to changing something in your life is to understand it, so here are a few tips to assist you on the journey towards a healthy relationship with anger:

1.   Accept that anger has its place.

One thing to remember is that anger is a useful emotion that has its place in our lives. Don't be afraid to follow your Inner Guidance when you are being called from a state of depression to one of anger. In such a case, you are making an improvement in the way you feel.

The unhealthiest emotion for you is that feeling of powerless depression or despair. However, many people are taught that it is better to run off and feel sorry for yourself than to get angry. Why? Because it is convenient for the person who doesn't want to witness your anger.

Depression, which often results from repressed anger, is actually anger in a new form. It is anger turned inwards. And that is the worst thing that you could do to yourself. So, allow yourself to feel anger, hatred, or even rage for a short while. Draw pictures of the

146

person and scratch their eyes out if you feel like it. Scream, yell, cry, or jump up and down. Have an angry pillow fight with your sofa. Do whatever you must do to honor and validate your own feelings, but plan to move on for your own benefit.

2.   Forgiveness is the answer.

Many people refuse to forgive because they feel that the other person does not deserve it. They hold a grudge as if it is somehow paying back the person with whom they are angry. However, forgiveness is not for the other person. You must let go and forgive so that you may live out your life purpose.

You came into this physical world to experience outrageous joy while using your powerfully creative thoughts to contribute to the expansion of our great Universe. And the ability to do so is always within you. Yes, you also have the ability to spend your entire life being angry, but this choice will create life experiences that are not in harmony with what you want.

3.   It is not what they did, but what you think about what they did.

Your feelings are not the result of anything outside of yourself, so do not hold anyone else responsible for them. The way that you feel is always a reflection of what you are thinking. If you are thinking angry thoughts that hold you away from that which your Inner Guidance is calling you towards, you will feel

147

bad. So, no matter what has happened, you remain in control of your reality. You are empowered to practice the art of allowing by releasing resistant thoughts and letting law of attraction deliver your ideal life. However, you are equally empowered to remain angry, thus using undesirable circumstances as an excuse to disallow the joyful life that is your birthright.

4.   Move rather than jump up the emotional scale.

You don't have to, and probably won't be able to, make a big jump from anger to joy. Be patient with yourself. If you've been thinking angry thoughts for a very long time, you will not be able to completely change this overnight. The important thing is just that you start making some improvements.

The law of attraction will send thoughts to match whatever you are thinking, so trust that you will have the support of the Universe as you guide your thoughts towards that which feels better. You may move up from anger to worry, from worry to disappointment, from disappointment to frustration, from frustration to hopefulness, from hopefulness to positive expectation, and from positive expectation to joy. It doesn't matter how many different emotions you experience on your journey, but you will notice life changing results at every step of the way. Keep your eyes open for small opportunities to appreciate and you will attract joy, happiness, love, and everything that you desire for your life.

5. It's all about your vibration.

Because the law of attraction is responding to the vibration of your thoughts, you are always in control. However, your thoughts need to be a "vibrational match" to your desires in order to experience the benefits of your creative power. Angry thoughts, which have a very low vibration, add resistance that prevents or delays manifestations. In other words, your anger towards a person or situation may cause you to have undesirable experiences in other areas of your life.

At any moment, however, you can choose to think about a situation differently or you can think about something else altogether. It only takes 68 seconds of focusing on a subject for the Universe to begin sending similar thoughts. And as you continue thinking thoughts that feel better, you will manifest circumstances that make it easier to think and feel great. This is how you create your reality.

If you allow angry thoughts to fester in your mind, realize that you are the one creating your misery. Also realize that you are fully empowered to change it when you are ready. You owe it to yourself to have thoughts that summon law of attraction in a non-resistant way, thus creating the life of your dreams.

⏻

CHAPTER 15: LIFE-CHANGE

Why is change important? Well without change there will be no progress, without progress there will be no movement, without movement there will be no growth, without growth there will be no development, without development there will be no events, without event there will be no time, without time there will be no space, without time and space there will no existence. Despite the importance of change we cannot help but resist change. Why is that? Well, we are far removed from our natural purpose in life which includes my reference of the I's of life; to live, to love, and to learn. Rather we live in a materialistic world, in a society where we are defined by career, status, class, sex, race, and age. We spend our lives trying to live up to the standards of society while losing focus on the purpose of life changes in our individual lives.

The direction of change follows an individual's purpose in life. Keep in mind that everyone has bad thoughts whether they are aware or not, but not everyone has good thoughts. Change can push us in the right or a wrong direction depending on our thoughts of purpose in life. I believe living life with a wholesome purpose is the best environment for change. Knowing our purpose in life is essential in understanding and accepting life changes, including steering our life in the right direction through our life choices.

There are a variety of reasons for this not being the case, one being that as we live longer, the changes usually are more impacting to our life and life meaning. The larger changes create a number of smaller losses and ripples in our world and many times we must grieve a cluster of losses all at one time. When life changes occur, such as a change in our roles, physical abilities, career, relationship or financial status, it can leave one feeling overwhelmed. These types of changes have a deeper meaning and impact on life and identity more than one would imagine.

It is true that the repetitive nature of having to deal with change may build basic resiliency and bring about an awareness of how to cope better, acquiring new emotional tools in our toolbox. For the larger or more significant changes, those skills may cease to work sufficiently. Here are some tips that may help.

•   Don't ignore the impact of the change. The sooner we accept the change has occurred and that it is real, the sooner we can begin to manage it.

•   If you find yourself uncertain why the impact of the change is affecting you at this level then there is something you have not seen. Is this coming on the back of a number of smaller changes, either associated with this one change or even unrelated? If not then the intensity is likely related to your self-image or the meaning held in maintaining what was.

•   Understand where your control lies. We often see the world as permanent and when it changes around us we may feel like any control we once felt has dissolved. We must shift our control from external to internal. You still have control over your thoughts beliefs and feelings. Putting your emphasis on these areas can help one feel more in control and therefore more resilient.

•   With all change comes some loss, but often there is also new opportunity. The new opportunity may not be apparent to you know, however, the belief that it is there, yet to be discovered is vitally important.

•   Life change is loss and therefore, we feel grief for what was. We must understand that grief takes time to get through; it doesn't happen overnight. Identity took a process to create so re-forging a broken identity takes a process, which requires time.

•   Shift your focus to what hasn't changed; what aspects of your life and identity have remained intact. What beliefs have not been shaken by recent events? Go beyond making a mental record; actually right the beliefs down. The action of writing things down, make them more tangible and therefore more concrete and emotionally accessible to us.

•   For the big losses, we may even need to rediscover who we are again. The example of spousal separation comes to mind when they have been a couple since young adulthood. In these cases, it can be helpful to go back to your essential self, the person you were prior to the relationship. What did you enjoy doing, who were your friends and why? What did you dream of doing back then that you never got to do? These are the types of questions we can begin to use to discover that essential self: the self we were becoming before our trajectory was changed by the other person's essential self.

• Surround yourself with people who are supportive and not negative minded. We have all kinds of relationships in our lives and not all are healthy or productive to be around when going through tough periods in our life. Sensor yourself from negative and fearful people.

• Monitor what type of television, radio programs, and even music you listen too. These things can bring added stress, anxiety and depressed feelings you don't need.

Some life changing events may require some additional assistance to get through. No matter how resilient we have been, there can be a change, or changes, that are just so shattering to our sense of safety in the world we need professional direction. If you are going through this type of life change, you likely do not need to work with someone weekly. Even 1-2 sessions per month can provide great benefit and make the difference in surviving or thriving through difficult life change.

The purpose of life changes is evident in our very existence, without change we would not exist. We experience life changes throughout our existence or lifetime and how these changes impact our lives depends on our individual purpose. When we live life with a wholesome purpose it is easier to accept change because we can understand the benefits of change. We may not like or understand the difficult twist and turns of change, however, knowing with a positive perspective that change is a part of life perhaps the purpose of life changes would outweigh the our resistance to change.▢

CONCLUSION

It should now be clear that anger can be expressed in many forms. It can be spoken in angry or sarcastic words. Nagging or quarelling are especially divisive forms of anger. It can be expressed in a mood like irritability or in the silence of pouting. It can also be physically demonstrated through violent actions. Revenge and hatred are often the most extreme forms of anger.

To allow oneself to exhibit any of these forms of anger is bad. It is a sign of a flaw in one's character and personality. More devastating than the effects on the person himself are the evil effects that anger can have on other people. Anger destroys harmony in the home. It can endanger peace in a neighborhood, a city, country, or even in the world. Angry people cause problems wherever they go – on the job, in a meeting, or at a party.

Anger is also a stumbling block on the road to perfection. For some people, it is just a small obstacle. For others, it is a major stumbling block. Either way, a person must work diligently each day and in every human situation to remedy this great problem of anger. With hard work and the ever-present assistance of friends, family and health professional, this problem can be remedied. Unnecessary and unreasonable anger can be stopped.

I hope that you found some of the ideas in this booklet useful. You can continue to use the techniques you found helpful long into the future and they should continue to benefit you. If some of the ideas are not particularly helpful at first, it is perhaps worth sticking with them for a few weeks to give them a chance to work. If however, you feel your situation remains largely unchanged or if you did not find this booklet useful, you should speak to a professional who can tell you about the other options available which you could find helpful.

46587872R00090

Made in the USA
Lexington, KY
28 July 2019